STANDING TOGETHER

IMPACTING YOUR GENERATION

HOWARD HENDRICKS

VISION™
HOUSE
PUBLISHING, INC.
Gresham, Oregon 97030

STANDING TOGETHER
© 1995 by Howard Hendricks

Published by Vision House Publishing Inc.
1217 NE Burnside Rd.
Suite 403
Gresham, Oregon 97030

Printed in the United States of America

Unless otherwise indicated, Scripture references are from the Holy Bible: New
International Version, copyright 1973, 1978, 1984 by the International Bible
Society. Used by permission of Zondervan Bible Publishers.

ISBN: 1-885305-31-1

95 96 97 98 99 00 01—08 07 06 05 04 03 02 01

"IF YOU ARE LIKE ME...

you can never get enough of Howard Hendricks. Both his speaking and his writing penetrate our generation like 'well driven nails.' His newest volume is vintage Hendricks: life-related themes set fourth in street-level talk. His words refuse to be ignored as they leap from the page and walk right into your heart. In a world marked by indecision and confusion, it's reassuring to witness a modern-day Elijah, who not only knows where he is going but invites us to travel with him. *STANDING TOGETHER* belongs at the top of your 'must read' list."

Charles R. Swindoll
President, Dallas Theological Seminary
Bible Teacher, Insight for Living

CONTENTS

Part One: Standing for the Truth

1. Conviction 9
2. Communion 19
3. Confrontation 33
4. Communication 49
5. Commitment 63
6. Confidence 77

Part Two: Serving Your Generation

7. Mentoring 93
8. Ministry 107
9. Mission 121
10. Maturity 137
11. Modeling 153
12. Multiplication 169

Part Three: Leaving a Legacy

13. Making a Difference,
    Impacting Lives 187

Acknowledgements 203

Standing
for the
Truth

CHAPTER ONE

Conviction

U p the palace steps runs the irate prophet. Past the astonished guards he storms. You can almost hear their jaws dropping: "Hey, where did this guy come from? Who let him in here?"

Sweeping like a wind through the dumbstruck court, the man of God rushes right into the throne room, and there confronts wicked King Ahab: "As the Lord, the God of Israel, lives, whom I serve, there will be neither dew nor rain in the next few years except at my word" (1 Kings 17:1).

With that, the determined dynamo turns on his heel and, as suddenly as he came, disappears, his mission accomplished—for the time being.

Thus we encounter the man Elijah. To appreciate why he undertook this explosive expedition, we must understand the times in which he lived. The nation of Israel was in moral free-fall. Its spirituality was seized by a mania of mediocrity. Most of the people had turned their backs on God—most especially King Ahab and his evil wife, Jezebel. Meanwhile, the relative handful of remaining God-fearers huddled miserably in a cave, apparently hiding from responsibility. "We don't want to get involved!" they seemed to be saying by their absence.

But one man refused to be cowed. Like a spiritual colossus towering over a generation of moral pygmies, Elijah held his ground for God.

It was not an easy task. First Kings 16 gives us the backdrop: "Ahab son of Omri did more evil in the eyes of the Lord than any of those before him. He not only considered it trivial to commit the sins of Jeroboam son of Nebat, but he also married Jezebel daughter of Ethbaal king of the Sidonians, and began to serve Baal and worship him. He set up an altar for Baal in the temple of Baal that he built in Samaria. Ahab also made an Asherah pole and did more to provoke the Lord, the God of Israel, to anger than did all the kings of Israel before him" (16:30–33).

In other words, Ahab shattered the record for rebellion. He not only turned away from God, he was anti-God. He *devoted* himself to idolatry and promoted it actively among the people. As a result, the culture began to crater, and it became neither comfortable nor convenient to take a stand for God in that generation. It never is! Yet Elijah dismissed comfort and convenience in order to bear witness to the God he served.

How does one come by such conviction? How does a person summon the courage to hold fast to faith even as the floodwaters of apostasy are sweeping others away? Where does a man find the sheer guts to face a godless king and tell him that God's judgment is at hand? Let's find out by observing Elijah's life and ministry. We'll see three key principles that we can put into practice in our own day.

Elijah was Convinced of the Reality of God

Notice the first recorded words of Elijah: "As the Lord, the God of Israel lives . . ." (17:1). God is alive, and the prophet recognized that fact. Ahab and his confederates thought they had successfully interred Jehovah-worship. But they made one serious miscalculation: they forgot one man. And that's all it takes in any society—one person wholly given over to the Lord, shot through with the reality that only God can bring into human experience.

Have you ever noticed that the most convincing thing about Christianity is its power to change people's lives? Nothing else in this world transforms in such a profound way. You can throw yourself into causes, campaigns, and praiseworthy activity, but nothing but Christ's power shapes your character toward righteousness.

And it is character that counts. The world is not impressed by our eloquent argumentation, nor is it convinced by our elaborate explanations. The world wants to see reality in a person's life. It only takes notice of that which it cannot produce—a life transformed by righteousness. But only God can produce that—which is why Christianity is the most revolutionary force in the world. It promises to effect true life-change.

So I ask, what is there in your life that you cannot explain on any other basis than the supernatural? What is there that is proof positive of the reality of God in your life? Please note: I'm not asking whether you believe that God exists. You no doubt do. In fact, most people in our society generally believe in a "higher power." But the question is, what *real changes* are being wrought in your life that demonstrate—to a world screaming for reality—that God is present in your life?

When my children were youngsters, I kept praying, "Lord, change my children." Nothing happened. Then I began to see that my prayers were misdirected. "Lord, change my children's father," I started praying. After God was pleased to do that, I saw remarkable changes in my children.

I remember one time I was to speak at a banquet on a Friday night. When I got home from the seminary where I teach and pulled in the driveway, my headlights fell on my son Bob's bicycle. For days it had been standing there in the carport, its rear tire flat as a pancake. I had promised to fix it, but I still hadn't followed through. I had a plane to catch early the next morning, so I decided it was now or never. I called Bob, grabbed the bike, and we patched that old tire. Then I washed up, grabbed a fresh shirt and a tie, and tore across town.

By the time I arrived at the banquet, I was only twenty minutes late, but the emcee had ulcers on top of his ulcers. "Where in the world have you been?" he asked anxiously.

"I'm awfully sorry," I said. "I had to fix a flat."

"I thought you had a new car!" he replied.

"Oh, I do. It was my boy's bike that had the flat."

Boom! That man lost it. He gave me a piece of his mind that he could ill afford to lose. He chewed me up one side and down the other, in effect saying I was wasting his and the dinner crowd's time by fiddling with my kid's bike. When he finally got through, I asked, "Did it ever occur to you, my friend, that it may be far more important for me to fix my boy's bicycle tire than to eat your meal?"

Not long after that, Bob and I were out in the park, playing ball together and throwing stones in the creek. I asked him, "Hey, Bob, do you love me?"

"I sure do, Dad," he replied.

"Great! How come?"

"Because you play ball with me and fix my bike tire!"

Can you see what matters? My kids were never impressed by the fact that I was a seminary professor. They never stood in awe of the several books that I've written, or of my worldwide travels. They were only impressed to the extent that Jesus Christ was a reality in my life. You see, I could easily pull the wool over your eyes in a book like this, but I could never pull the wool over the eyes of my wife and children. They know what I'm like—warts and all. The same is true for you. Those closest to you will inevitably recognize how real God is in your life.

So how do you convince them that God is alive? By revealing His life through your own. When His power changes your life, you have a genuine message for a phony generation.

Elijah Was Convinced He Was a Representative of God

But Elijah tells us something else: "As the Lord, the God of Israel, lives, *whom I serve* . . ." (17:1, emphasis added). Elijah was a servant. My friend, that lends dignity to Christian experience. I never cease to be amazed at how God consistently performs the miracle of ministry by employing human personalities to accomplish divine purposes. That makes us personal representatives of the living God.

Unfortunately, however, while our generation is screaming for answers, too many Christians are stuttering. While all the world is grasping for an outstretched hand, too many Christians are paralyzed. Many of us seem both unable and unwilling to offer the only answer there is to the most searching questions people ask. And others of us are throwing up our hands in despair. "What can we do?" we cry to ourselves. "It's hopeless! The nation is doomed!"

I am quite sure that Elijah could have come to the same conclusion. The leadership of his day was corrupt. The masses were aimless. The glory of Israel was long gone. Yet what was Elijah's perspective? "I am a servant of the Lord!"

Do you know how God always responds to a crisis? He calls an individual into His service. That was true then; it is still true today. God is always looking for one person who will serve as His personal representative. Not just in the pulpit, or on the mission field, or as a teacher in a church. He calls some to those strategic venues. But God is calling people from all walks of life to represent Him everywhere in the world—in neighborhoods and communities, in offices and factories, in homes and on campuses, all across the world. In fact, He is calling *you* to stand for

Him in one of the myriad places where people are blind to His reality. He wants them to see His life incarnate in you.

Let me speak about this from my own experience. I have to confess that, like many vocational Christian workers, I have been prone to become compulsively active. Perhaps you're familiar with the syndrome. The "barrenness of busy-ness," I call it. Activity becomes an anesthetic to deaden the pain of an empty life. But it's activity without accomplishment.

In my case, I've had periods in my life when I would get up in the morning and run down a laundry list of "Christian things" to be done. I'd say to myself, "Okay, I've got to have my devotions today, I've got to go to work, I've got to spend time with Jeanne and the kids, I've got to witness . . ." On and on and on. I was quite active—but my experience was sterile.

Then I returned to the truth that Elijah recognized: I am God's servant! He wants me to be *available* to Him, as His messenger boy, ready to do what He asks, so as to accomplish His purposes. When I began to start my mornings by asking, "Lord, what would *You* have me do today?" then my days were no longer filled with meaningless activity. Everything began to take on significance. Seeing myself as God's representative has revitalized my walk with Christ.

I'll never forget the time I had a week of meetings in which I spoke thirty-four times in eight days. I must have been crazy! At any rate, right after the last meeting I hopped on a plane in Chicago bound for Los Angeles. I walked all the way to the back and grabbed a window seat on a vacant row, praying, "Lord, don't send anyone to sit beside me. I'm dog tired, and I can't take one more person."

Well, that plane filled up—but nobody sat next to me. Finally, they were closing the door, and I thought, "I'm home free!" But then I looked up and saw a GI heading down the aisle. You guessed it: there was only one empty seat left—the one next to me. He plopped down beside me and started to talk. And talk. And talk some more. I mean, that boy must have been vaccinated with a phonograph needle! He told me he'd been waiting for a flight all night and all day. He'd been bumped nineteen times before they finally put him on a plane!

He went on and on, telling me his story. But eventually he must have started to run out of gas, because he asked me the question, "By the way, sir, what do you do?"

That is always a slightly embarrassing question for me. People tend to have a lot of stereotypes about ministers in general, and seminary professors in particular. In fact, I usually make good progress in a conversation until somebody asks that question. Then I start falling all over myself.

"I'm in education," I replied, telling the truth—but not exactly the whole truth.

"Oh, that's interesting," the soldier countered. "Where do you teach?"

"Dallas Theological Seminary," I mumbled, sort of swallowing the last two words. I could tell by the look on his face that he was trying to figure out just what sort of institution this was. Then he finally hit on it.

"Oh, I got it!" he cried. "You're a preacher!"

"Yeah," I admitted, "I'm a preacher."

Then I got the surprise of my life. Instead of tuning me out or changing the subject, that young man said to me, "Sir, after I visit home, I'm on my way to Vietnam. I'm not supposed to be scared, but I gotta tell you—I'm scared to death! You got anything to help me?"

Don't you just love the way God sometimes rearranges your agenda? I pulled out my New Testament and explained the gospel to him. Then, probably somewhere over Denver, he prayed to receive Christ as his Savior.

When we landed in Los Angeles and were getting off the plane, I said, "Hey, friend, I want you to do me a favor. I'm going to write my name and number on a card, and when you get to Nam, I want you to drop me a line. I'll send you some literature that will help you build on this new foundation of Jesus Christ."

Three weeks later, this boy lands in Vietnam. He walks into his barracks, and the first order his sergeant gives him is to attend chapel. So he goes, and the chaplain gives a gospel message. The kid is thinking to himself, "That's the same stuff that guy on the plane was talking about." So after the service, he goes up to the chaplain and tells him all about his plane ride seated next to a guy named Hendricks, and about his decision to trust Christ. And the chaplain says, "Hendricks? He was my professor at seminary!" And the chaplain began to tell that baby Christian what he needed to know about growing in his faith.

Now some people might say, "My, what an amazing story. A kid happens to be bumped nineteen times, finally gets on a plane, and just happens to sit next to the teacher of his Army chaplain. Quite a coincidence!"

But that was no coincidence. I know it wasn't, because I know that God has a plan for me, just as He had a plan for that young soldier (and for you, too). Like Elijah, I know that I'm a servant of the Most High, and part of my role is to wake up each day saying, "Lord, I'm just your suit of clothes. Put me on and wear me around and accomplish your purposes in any way you see fit."

Elijah Was Convinced He Had the Resources of God

The final thing that Elijah told Ahab was that it wasn't going to rain anymore apart from Elijah's say-so. Now how could that be? Was Elijah some kind of magician? No, James in the New Testament tells us plainly, "Elijah was a man just like us." Think of that: Elijah was just like us!

But James goes on to say, "He prayed earnestly that it would not rain, and it did not rain on the land for three and a half years" (James

5:17). Where did Elijah find the courage to confront the king? I believe it was a product of his prayer life. Thanks to prayer, Elijah developed a solid conviction about the reality and resources of God. Thus he was able to trust that the Lord would do what He promised.

What had God promised? In Deuteronomy 11:16–17, God had warned His people Israel, "Be careful, or you will be enticed to turn away and worship other gods and bow down to them. Then the Lord's anger will burn against you, and he will shut the heavens so that it will not rain and the ground will yield no produce, and you will soon perish from the good land the Lord is giving you."

That was God's covenant: idolatry would lead to drought. Ahab and the people had forgotten that commitment. Elijah had not. He was convinced that God would keep His word by withholding rain from the rebellious nation. He also knew that what the Lord had promised, He was able to perform. Consequently, this man took a stand for righteousness and, according to James, prayed earnestly for God to stop the rains. God answered his prayer.

Today our world is soaked in sin, yet starving for truth. Thinking itself wise, our culture has largely turned away from the one true God. On every hand, people give themselves over to the foolish idols of selfish pleasure. In the midst of this moral wasteland, do you recognize the resources that are available to you from the Lord? You have everything Elijah had, and more: the Word of God, the Spirit of God, the power of prayer. What more do you need? Can you believe God for what He says in Scripture, and then pray that He will perform His promises? Prayer and faith. Those are the tools Elijah used to impact his society for the Almighty. You can use them in much the same way.

I experienced something of that a few years ago—frankly, in a way that I hope I never have to experience again. I was in a prayer meeting made up of pastors, and the unbelief was so crass, I had to get up and walk out. Instead of praying, those gathered were all caught up in comparing their ministries and boasting of their accomplishments. There was talk of marketing and money—but no one was crying out for God to reveal Himself in a powerful way to our sin-saturated society.

Finally, I left the group and went back to my room and began to read my Bible, filling my mind with God's promises. As I did so, I realized afresh that I am nothing but His representative, just one of His servants. But that means that all the resources available to Elijah—and to any other individual of faith—are certainly available to me, too. So I began to pray for the impossible—that the Lord would change hearts in that "prayer" meeting. Do you know that God worked a miracle! The entire focus of the group was transformed by the quiet working of the Holy Spirit.

The power to change the world is available to all of us. At any moment, in any situation, we can appropriate God's resources through His Word and the prayer of faith. We can watch God perform miracles in our world and in the lives of people around us.

The question, then, is whether you are a person with godly conviction? Is the Lord a living reality in your experience? Like Elijah, do you perceive yourself as God's representative, to be used by Him as He sees fit? And do you live with the deep conviction that God's resources are available at any moment? If so, then take your stand, and let God work through you to impact your generation.

CHAPTER TWO

Communion

Chad Walsh, in his intriguing book *Early Christians of the Twenty-First Century*, placed a burr in my mental saddle with these words:

> Millions of Christians live in a sentimental haze of vague piety, with soft organ music trembling in the lovely light from stained-glass windows. Their religion is a pleasant thing of emotional quivers, divorced from the will, divorced from the intellect, and demanding little except lip service to a few harmless platitudes. I suspect that Satan has called off his attempt to convert people to agnosticism. After all, if a man travels far enough away from Christianity, he is liable to see it in perspective and decide that it is true. It is much safer, from Satan's point of view, to vaccinate a man with a mild case of Christianity so as to protect him from the real disease.

Perhaps you know the sort of person Walsh is describing. Theirs is an easy theology, the sort that has become very popular in our culture. They cozy up to all the "nice" parts of God—His love, mercy, and forgiveness—but conveniently forget about the inconvenient parts of His character—justice, wrath, and holiness. They are quick to insist that "God is love," but forget that Scripture also declares that He is "holy, holy, holy." They love to tell the story of Jesus forgiving the woman caught in adultery, but they shy away from the Lord's punch line in that encounter: "Go and sin no more!"

People who live this sort of shallow spirituality come across as phony. They may act as though they know the deep truths of God, but it's all a façade. Faced with a crisis, their faith cannot sustain them. You see, Jesus didn't just talk about forgiving people of their sin—*He died to take their sin away!* And the reason Christ was willing to lay down His life for the truth was because He knew what was true, and He remained close to His Father, the one true God.

There is nothing as repulsive as phoniness in the spiritual realm. Conversely there is nothing as magnetic as reality. A person of truth is attractive, drawing others to the truth. So with all the spiritual charlatans in this world, how refreshing to encounter a man who was genuine— Elijah. There was not a shred of hypocrisy in his life or experience. Problems, yes. Phoniness, no.

In the last chapter we explored the convictions of Elijah. This rustic renegade from the rural regions burst into Ahab's palace and delivered an ultimatum to the king. He had the courage to speak out to a generation in spiritual decline because he was a man of conviction. He was convinced that God was still very much alive and had sent him as His personal representative to his society. That created a responsibility to speak out while others were hiding. Elijah became the preeminent spokesman for righteousness, even though speaking out placed him at great peril.

But notice what happened after Elijah stormed out of Ahab's

presence? He retreated from the center of the action into solitude. A careful reading of 1 Kings 17:2–7 reveals a cause-and-effect relationship. Show me an individual who is effective in public, and I will show you an individual who is effective in private. Find a person of deep conviction who is genuinely impacting his society, and you'll inevitably find a person who spends time alone with God.

This is why people of shallow faith cannot change their world. They fail to commune with the Lord one on one. Consequently, they lack the conviction to speak for Him when faced with an audience. I meet many young people who aspire to a prominent position from which to serve God. They see front-line action as heroic. But they fail to take into account the fact that every hero of faith has spent considerable time in his prayer closet before striding forth to do battle with Satan.

There are four words that unravel the plot of 1 Kings 17:2–7: command, promise, response, and test. The order is both significant and spiritual. God gives a command; with it, He makes a promise; He awaits our response; and then He puts our decision to the test. That is exactly the pattern of Elijah.

The Command

The account begins, "Then the word of the Lord came to Elijah: 'Leave here, turn eastward and hide in the ravine of Kerith, east of the Jordan'" (1 Kings 17:2–3).

Can you imagine that? Elijah must have thought, "*Hide* myself, Lord? *Now?* Right when we've got Ahab on the ropes? Right when there is so much to be done and so few people doing it? You want me to go and hide out?"

Often our ego doesn't want to hide. It wants to star. When God says, "Go show yourself," we rejoice. But when He tells us, "Go hide," we reply, "Huh?" That's what I would have done had I been in Elijah's place. I would have argued with God. "Lord, are you sure we don't have a wire crossed somewhere? I mean, I'm a palace man. You don't want a palace man hiding himself in the rocks, do You?" I might have even rationalized myself into *avoiding* a retreat: "I must have misunderstood you, Lord. I know You would never call me to someplace remote like that."

I'm convinced that there are many Christians today to whom God is saying, "Go and hide yourself." That can be a difficult assignment in a busy world. As I mentioned earlier, many of us are compulsive activists, busy every moment. And there are so many voices clamoring for our attention that it is easy to miss the voice of the Lord.

You may be asking God to use you, shape you, mold you, and give you a cutting edge. You may very well be entreating the Lord to use you not only in the present generation but, if He tarries, in the next. But you will have nothing to say to any generation unless God first speaks to you.

God knew that about Elijah. To be the leader God wanted him to be, Elijah had to spend time alone, quietly listening to the Lord. If he was going to be effective, he could not rely on his own words or strength. He needed the resources of the Almighty. And there was only one way to accumulate those: spending time in seclusion with God.

The Lord Jesus followed the same pattern. He often went off by Himself, away from the crowds and the excitement of His ministry, just to hide with the heavenly Father.

If that was necessary for Him, how much more for you? The important thing in your walk with Christ is not what you read or what you hear in a sermon or a seminar. As important as those teachings can be, they are simply instruments in the hands of God. In the final analysis, what matters is whether you are listening to God Himself. If you are not hearing from Him, if you are not cultivating an intimate relationship with Him, then the words of others will make little sense, and their message will have little impact on your life.

I was speaking at a conference some years ago, and I talked with a man who came to see me for counsel. He was facing severe problems in his work, and found it difficult to stay on top of it all. I asked him,

"Friend, how much time do you spend thinking?"

"Thinking?" he replied. "Hendricks, I don't have any time to think. If I stop to think, I get behind!".

That's precisely our dilemma.

During the fourth century, Julian the Apostate was determined to blot out every trace of Christianity. He discovered to his embarrassment the law of spiritual thermodynamics: the greater the heat, the more the expansion. The more he persecuted Christianity, the more it flourished. Finally, he gathered his remaining band of followers in an upper room and shouted, "Bah! Christianity provokes too much thinking. Why, even the slaves are thinking!" This, to a Roman mind, was incredible. But it was true; even slaves were now thinking under the impact of the Word of God.

Do you spend time thinking? Do you spend time meditating on the Word of God, exploring its message, and waiting for the Lord to speak to you? I have never met a Christian who sat down and planned to live a mediocre life. But if most of us keep going in the direction we're headed, we may end up there. Long ago, Plato observed that the unexamined life is not worth living. That is especially true for Christians. Believers who never take the time to bring themselves into the presence of God will never hear His voice. "Go and hide yourself," God says. How willing are you to obey Him?

The Promise

God never gives a command without providing the dynamic to fulfill that command. He never calls us to a task without providing the resources needed to accomplish it. "You will drink from the brook," He explained to Elijah, "and I have ordered the ravens to feed you there" (17:4).

The promised fare was simple, but sufficient. It was enough to take care of Elijah, and to meet his needs as he prepared for the work to which he had been called. If we are going to have communion with God, we must trust that He will care for our needs.

I have wonderful opportunities working with students. I recall one young man who came to see me periodically. He had spent time alone with God, and now he was dreaming dreams and seeing visions. Whenever I met with him, I thought, "If I can just keep him away from some of these older Christians who'll want to throw a wet blanket on what God is leading him to do, we may hear from this fellow before long." If I were to tell you what he had in mind, you might well snicker, his idea appeared so outrageous. But he had been planning and thinking and praying about this work, and he was convinced that God wanted him to do great things.

One day he came to me and said, "Prof, there are a lot of problems. God is going to have to do a miracle if we're ever going to get this thing off the ground."

"Wonderful," I replied, "God specializes in miracles. Did it ever occur to you that there is not a significant work in our day that has not been the product of a miracle-working God?"

Then I reminded this student of the experience of Dallas Seminary. Shortly after the seminary was founded in 1924, it almost folded. It came to the point of bankruptcy. All the creditors were ready to foreclose at twelve noon on a particular day. That morning, the founders of the school met in the president's office to pray that God would provide. In that prayer meeting was Harry Ironside. When it was his turn to pray, he said in his refreshingly candid way, "Lord, we know that the cattle on a thousand hills are Thine. Please sell some of them and send us the money."

Just about that time, a tall Texan in boots and an open-collar shirt strolled into the business office. "Howdy!" he said to the secretary. "I just sold two carloads of cattle over in Fort Worth. I've been trying to make a business deal go through, but it just won't work. I feel God wants me to give this money to the seminary. I don't know if you need it or not, but here's the check," and he handed it over.

The secretary took the check and, knowing something of the critical nature of the hour, went to the door of the prayer meeting and timidly tapped. Dr. Lewis Sperry Chafer, the founder and president of the school, answered the door and took the check from her hand. When he looked at the amount, it was for the exact sum of the debt. Then he recognized the name on the check as that of the cattleman. Turning to Dr. Ironside, he said, "Harry, God sold the cattle."

Often the Lord provides for us in ways we would never have expected. Sometimes it is difficult to see how He plans to meet our needs. Certainly Elijah never expected to be called to the wilderness, or to have his food brought to him by the birds. But the very nature of God's provision built his faith, and must have helped him understand the Lord even more. That's what communion with God does in your life.

Are you dreaming dreams and seeing visions? Is the Spirit of God moving in your life with concern to reach those around you who don't know Jesus Christ? Is He stirring you up to accomplish something important in your world? If that is not your experience, then perhaps you need to be reintroduced to the God Elijah knew intimately. Perhaps you need to refresh your relationship with the One who says, "Go off by yourself. I will feed you. I will give you drink."

The Response

God told Elijah to withdraw, and what was the prophet's response? "So he did what the Lord had told him. He went to the ravine of Kerith, east of the Jordan, and stayed there. The ravens brought him bread and meat in the morning and bread and meat in the evening, and he drank from the brook" (17:5–6).

My heart leaps at these words because they are in such contrast to my own experience. If I had been in Elijah's shoes, I suspect I might have gotten into an argument with God. I would have listed all the reasons why I was sure that He was making a mistake. I would have presented a few choice ideas to "improve" on His plan. And I also might have lectured Him a bit on the proper treatment of "spiritual luminaries."

But that's not what Elijah did. He simply "did what the Lord had told him." That response of obedience was crucial if Elijah hoped to enjoy intimate communion with his God. You see, obedience reveals an attitude of trust and a teachable spirit.

That attitude is evident throughout the rest of 1 Kings 17, which tells of Elijah following the Lord's instruction. Confident in God's promise to care for him, Elijah goes to the widow of Zaraphath and is used of God to miraculously provide for her needs during the famine.

We have a similar instance of God sending one of his servants on an errand in Acts 9. As the chapter opens, we are introduced to Saul, "breathing out murderous threats" against the early church. But while en route from Jerusalem to Damascus, Saul meets the risen Christ and undergoes a spiritual transformation. However, the Christians had a hard time buying that. As far as they were concerned, he was still Public Enemy Number One. Saul went on to Damascus, as we'll see in a moment, but he eventually returned to Jerusalem. When he did, the account says that "he tried to join the disciples, but they were all afraid of him, not believing that he really was a disciple" (Acts 9:26). I can almost hear one of them saying, "Hey, how dumb does he think we are? He's feigning conversion in order to get on the inside of this group. That way he can identify all the believers and liquidate us one by one! No way are we taking him in!"

It's kind of hard to relate to this in contemporary Christianity. Today, we tend to throw open the doors of the church and suggestively ask people, "You do know Jesus as Savior—*don't you?*" Of course, anybody with a couple of brain cells functioning can figure out the right answer. As a result, we end up mingling a lot of unbelievers with the community of faith. But in Saul's day, Christians understood the importance of being careful. Sometimes their very lives depended on it.

This cautionary bias comes into play as soon as the new convert Saul arrived in Damascus. Literally blinded by his encounter with Jesus, he is conducted to a certain house and told to wait there for the Lord to send someone. That someone was a man named Ananias. I love to read the account of how God called this fellow to minister to Saul. It is so refreshingly real. The writer paints a brilliant picture of a person struggling with how to respond.

"In Damascus there was a disciple named Ananias" verse 10 begins. "The Lord called to him in a vision, 'Ananias!'"

Can't you just imagine the setting? There's Ananias, minding his own business. Then one day, out of the blue, the Lord calls him by name. Fortunately, Ananias recognizes the Lord's voice, and he answers, "Yes, Lord."

So the Lord begins to give him an assignment, and you get the sense that Ananias is only too willing. "Sure, Lord, whatever you want."

So the Lord draws him a map. "Go to the house of Judas . . ."

"Right!"

"on Straight Street . . ."

"Got it!"

"and ask for a man . . ."

"A man. Okay!"

"from Tarsus . . ."

"Man from Tarsus. Right!"

"named Saul."

"(Long pause) Huh?!"

I don't think Ananias heard a word from there on out. Notice his reply. It's a little prayer in which he offers God some advice: "Lord . . . I have heard many reports about this man and all the harm he has done to your saints in Jerusalem." (I guess he thought God hadn't yet heard the news about that!) "And he has come here with authority from the chief priests to arrest all who call on your name" (9:13–14). In other words, Ananias more or less asks, "Lord, are you sure you've got all of the facts here?"

But God interrupts Ananias with a simple command, "Go!" (9:15). To his credit, Ananias decides to do what he is told, and he goes and lays hands on Saul. He even calls him "brother" (9:17), which shows that he accepted Saul as a true convert. But how would you like that assignment: show up at the hotel room of Mr. Big, look around at all his cronies, then give him a big hug and say, "Welcome to the family, brother!"? It's a sure bet that Ananias was going through a Maalox moment!

Elijah would have a similar moment—but not yet. For now, God told the man who had been so successful before the king to go on a campout by a tiny, out of the way brook called Kerith. Just drop out for a while! There was not a word of argument from the prophet. He did exactly and immediately what the Lord told him.

That's the response God is looking for. You see, the opposite of ignorance in the spiritual realm is not knowledge—it's obedience. That's why Scripture says, "To *obey* is better than sacrifice, and to *heed* is better than the fat of rams" (1 Samuel 15:22, emphasis added). God is not impressed with our pretense of worship. He wants to know, will we practice His Word?

The Lord and I have a running argument. I constantly attempt to impress him with how much I know. He constantly seeks to impress me with how little I have obeyed. If you really want to find yourself in communion with God, obey Him. You'll discover, that's the response that opens the door to a deeper walk.

The Test

A command to go into the wilderness, the promise of God's supply, and a response of obedience on the part of the prophet. But now comes the real test of Elijah's faith. The account tells us, "Some time later the brook dried up because there had been no rain in the land" (1 Kings 17:7).

What a revolting development that must have been! Here was Elijah, obeying the Lord, both in public and in private, trusting His promises. And now his one source of water has dried up. If it were me, I'd be asking some serious questions. "Look, Lord, you're the One who told me to come here in the first place! I did exactly what you asked. So now that I'm right in the center of your will, what's the idea of shutting off the water? What's going on here?"

What's going in is that God is not interested simply in the impartation of faith—He is just as interested in the *development* of faith as well. And He knows that deep, abiding faith only develops under pressure. It takes a crucible to form diamonds in a human's character.

That was certainly the experience of Abraham. The Lord called him out from Ur of the Chaldees, led him across the Fertile Crescent, and down into the Promised Land. But he no sooner arrived there— smack dab in the center of God's will—than a severe famine gripped the land. So Abraham headed down to Egypt, where he found an even greater pack of trouble. Then when he got back to Canaan, the Lord tested him again by asking him to sacrifice his only, long-awaited son. From the human perspective, you think, "What gives?" But from the divine point of view, you realize that it was through testing that Abraham matured in his faith and drew close to God.

I've seen the same process at work in the lives of my seminary students. A young guy, extremely gifted, senses God calling him to the vocational ministry, so he enters the seminary for training. But by the end of his third week, his outlook is pretty rugged. He still hasn't found a job, his wife is sick, and he's just received back three exams, all marked with a big, fat "F." And while he hasn't learned much Greek yet, he knows enough English to realize the "F" doesn't stand for "fine"!

I've seen that student, clutching his tests in his hand, stand in my office and ask, "Prof, what happened? I've never been more convinced that I'm exactly where God wants me, but my life is in tatters."

And I respond, "My friend, what you are going through is as much a part of the curriculum as the courses in which you are enrolled. See, this is the curriculum God has designed—to shape you and mold you into the person He can use. These are the real tests, the ones that are going to mature you and build your confidence and understanding of God."

Our Lord illustrated this principle in Mark 4. The passage gives us a portion of the Master's teacher-training program as He attempted to groom a handful of men for a ministry of multiplication. First he told them a series of parables that focused on the subject of faith. But the Lord knew that people don't learn faith from a lecture. They learn faith in the laboratory of life. Jesus was a great teacher. He gave examinations—though not the kind we give in schools. Our approach to exams is to see how much of the material the student can cram into his bean and retain overnight. By contrast, the Lord used lifestyle learning to test the response of his learners. He wanted to see whether they would put His principles into practice.

The account begins, "That day . . ." (Mark 4:35), and immediately we are forced to ask, *which* day? Why, the same day on which the disciples had heard Christ lecturing about faith! It was on *that* day that "He said to His disciples, 'Let us go over to the other side'" (4:35). So they took off in a fishing boat across the water. But "a furious squall came up, and the waves broke over the boat, so that it was nearly swamped" (4:37).

Now remember, these men were professional fishermen. They were familiar with such storms, and their response shows that they realized they were in grave danger. So they hurried to Jesus, who, interestingly enough, was asleep in the back of the boat. "Teacher, don't you care if we drown?" they asked (4:38)—implying that Christ had somehow failed in his responsibility. So Jesus rebuked the wind and waves, and suddenly the sea was quiet.

Then the Lord asked them, "Why are you so afraid? Do you still have no faith?" (4:40). To translate the text literally, Jesus was saying, "How is it that *you*, of all people, have no faith? *You*—who just heard my lecture on faith. You all get an 'F' on this exam—and it doesn't stand for 'faith!'"

The Lord often tests those whom He has called by asking them to do something special. If it had not been for hard lessons like the storm on Galilee, Jesus' disciples would never have been prepared for the far tougher times that they would face later on, after Jesus returned to His Father.

I sometimes ask myself, what would Jesus say to me, or to my family, or to our church congregation, or to the faculty at the seminary? Is it possible that He might be forced question our faith? Might He be forced to ask us, "How is it that *you*, of all people, have no faith?"

I especially think about this in light of all the resources God has given us. You know, privilege creates responsibility, and God has graciously blessed many of us who are Christians in the West with so many freedoms, and so many advantages, and so many resources. I sometimes wonder if being a Christian has become too easy. One time I heard a group of believers whining about their church's air conditioning—completely forgetting that in many places, churches have no air conditioning. They don't even have a building! In fact, in some cultures, just congregating with other Christians is to take your life in your hands. So we need to allow the tests to bring perspective to our lives. We need to learn faith from them.

And they will come! God has commanded. He has promised. The next step is ours—we are to obey His command. But mark it well: the moment we take a significant step of obedience, we set ourselves up to be tested. Sooner or later, we'll be given an exam on faith.

Perhaps you're under testing right now. Perhaps you are sitting by a drying brook. You've obeyed God, and now it seems as though all the circumstances are against you. It could be a financial problem, or maybe a physical one. It could be emotional, intellectual, spiritual. And you are asking, "Lord, what is happening?"

"Nothing!" God may be saying. "I'm just answering your prayers."

Let's go back to Elijah. There he sits while his brook diminishes. It slows to a trickle, then a puddle, and finally it evaporates completely. God has promised to take care of him. But now he is out of water. How does he respond to this new wrinkle? I have the highest respect for Elijah, because I would not have been able to sit and watch that brook diminish. I would have gotten out my road map and started searching for the nearest watering hole. My motto would have been, "Don't Just Sit There—*Do Something!*"

But what does Elijah do? He sits there—by the dried up brook. Perhaps he wondered why God had called him to this arid place. Then suddenly, he remembered his prayer: "He prayed earnestly that it would not rain, and it did not rain on the land for three and a half years" (James 5:17). Aha! Elijah himself had asked for this!

Sometimes we pray, "Father, make me like your Son." So He takes us at our word and begins the process. Then we come back and complain, "Lord, what happened? Why did you allow all these bad things to come into my life? I was fine until all this stuff came up. What are you doing?" And He patiently replies, "Answering your prayers."

Friend, never forget that Jesus Christ, "although He was a son, learned obedience from what He suffered" (Hebrews 5:8). Perhaps the Holy Spirit is saying to you, "I really want to minister through you. But before I can minister through you, I must minister to you." Therefore, do not despise the educational experience of your drying brook. God wants to make you like His Son. But to do that, He must put you through the same process of learning-through-suffering that Jesus went through.

Listen to the command of God. Trust in His promises. Obey His commands and call. And hold fast to Him during times of testing. These are the steps to a deeper walk with God—the footsteps traced for us by Elijah, His servant.

CHAPTER THREE

Confrontation

God's processes invariably involve a person. When He needed an ark built, He chose a person. When He needed to rescue His people from Pharaoh, He chose a person. Whenever the Lord has an important work to be done, He chooses the right person for the job.

What kind of person does the Almighty choose to use? Well, His choice is often the exact opposite of human choice. Humans choose on the basis of externals—how a person appears. God chooses on the basis of internals—the character of the individual. Man chooses on the basis of what an individual is. God chooses on the basis of what an individual is to become. Elijah, sitting by a drying brook, is in the process of becoming. God has been ministering to him, drawing Elijah close to Himself. Now God is going to minister through him, using Elijah as His tool to accomplish His purpose.

There is perhaps no more dramatic scene in all of Scripture than the contest on Mount Carmel in 1 Kings 18. I wish I were an artist and could render the scene. Two explosive personalities collide, and the moment they do, sparks fly. Elijah is again sent by God to confront King Ahab, and the king greets him with an insult: "Is that you, the troubler of Israel?" (1 Kings 18:17). But Elijah is equal to the occasion. Like Nathan the prophet, he points his finger and says, "*You* are the man who has made trouble for Israel." He excoriates Ahab for his sin, and in doing so throws down the gauntlet.

There is no question in my mind who is in charge in this situation. Several times in this passage, Elijah takes the initiative. He is the one issuing commands and taking leadership. He challenged the king and the prophets of Baal and Asherah to a duel: in front of all the people, they were going to see whose god was the true God. The events that transpired that day offer some of the most telling insights into the believer's behavior during confrontation.

The day was proclaimed a national holiday in Israel. You can almost see the crowds streaming to the top of Mount Carmel, with its commanding view of the Mediterranean Sea. They were climbing up by every available route to witness a battle of the gods—fifteen rounds, winner take all!

What a scene of contrasts! On the one side are gathered the overwhelming majority of the people, rooting for the 850 prophets of Baal and Asherah. These leaders are clad in expensive, beautifully colored garments. Around each neck hangs a piece of metal deliberately crafted to catch and reflect the rays of the sun—for they worshiped the sun. Soon, the multitudes part for the grand entry of the king, borne on a litter by his retinue of servants, resplendent in his regal garments.

Then the eye shifts to the other side. There one finds a lone, gaunt man, crudely clothed, coarse in appearance, hair disheveled, eyes like steel. Someone says, "Isn't it a shame? He looks so lonely." But don't feel sorry for Elijah. He knows that God is more concerned with the internal temperature of a person than with the external trappings. Elijah makes seven statements that both unfold the story and provide practical lessons for Christians today who face spiritual confrontation.

1. Choose

Like a kickoff in a football game, Elijah launches the contest by confronting the people with a pointed question: "How long will you waver between two opinions? If the Lord is God, follow Him; but if Baal is God, follow him" (18:21). Thus he scores the people for their indecisiveness. In effect, he brings them to a fork in the road: "You're going to have to make a decision."

The spineless wavering of these people reminds me of the politician who, when asked his position on an issue, replied, "Well, some of my friends are for it, and some of my friends are against it. And I'm for my friends!" Elijah was determined that these people not emerge from the day with their feet still firmly planted in midair. So he told them, "Look, you've been straddling the fence long enough. There's no room here for peaceful coexistence. It's either Baal or Jehovah. Make up your minds!" His words stunned them into silence.

Many people in our world want to straddle the spiritual fence. They believe in God—but not enough to make their lives inconvenient. In fact, many of them aren't even saddened by a friend who joins the Mormon church, or a family member who gets involved with the Jehovah's Witnesses. "There must be something good to it," they rationalize. "It helped them with their problems."

But the fact remains that this world is a spiritual battlefield. It can never be "good" for someone to turn his life over to a falsehood, no matter what sort of short-term "good" it appears to offer. A lie is a lie, and sugar-coating it to make it more palatable won't turn it into a truth. When faced with a confrontation in the spiritual realm, we must first choose who we are going to believe: God or someone else. Obviously we need to be polite and speak the truth in love. But at some point we must take a stand for truth. As Elijah said, we must "choose this day whom we will serve."

2. Stand

Elijah's second statement further underscores Israel's problem: "I am the only one of the Lord's prophets left" (18:22). Later we find out that that was not exactly the case. But Elijah didn't know that, and he was willing to stand alone for God, even in front of a hostile crowd. How different in our day! It is so easy to be a Christian in our culture that I sometimes worry what even the smallest persecution might bring. Most of us have never had to face the hostility that Christians throughout much of the world face. I fear we may have become weak because of it.

For instance, how many times have you found yourself toning down your Christian message because you didn't want to "offend" anyone? That was not the case with Elijah. Coming against a multitude of hostile zealots who were cheered on by a throng of gutless accommodaters, the prophet unapologetically announced, "I stand for God!"

Then he set the terms of the contest: "You call on the name of your god, and I will call on the name of the Lord. The god who answers by fire—he is God" (18:24). Now that was a stroke of genius. Baal was the chief deity in the Canaanite pantheon of gods, and he was considered lord of the heavens. Whenever the priests of Baal saw lightning in the sky and heard thunder, they would exclaim, "That is Baal. That is god!" He was the lord of fire. So if the god of fire ought to be able to do anything, it's light a fire, right? Elijah was forcing them to put their god to the test.

The people thought that was a good idea. It was a very equitable arrangement. In fact, it was decidedly in their favor, since theirs was the "god of fire."

3. Faith

Having established the terms, Elijah said, in effect, "You go first." "Choose one of the bulls and prepare it. . . Call on the name of your god, but do not light the fire" (18:25). They did, and all morning they performed their idolatrous dances around their altar and chanted monotonously, "O Baal, answer us!" But as the text pointedly observes, "There was no response; no one answered" (18:26).

The Bible tells us that false gods "have mouths, but cannot speak, eyes, but they cannot see; they have ears, but cannot hear, noses, but they cannot smell; they have hands, but cannot feel, feet, but they cannot walk; nor can they utter a sound with their throats" (Psalm 115:5–8). On Mount Carmel that morning there is a dreadful silence. Oh yes, there is pandemonium as the priests of Baal leap and dance and shout. But the skies remain silent. Apparently Baal, the god of thunder, is speechless.

Then, when the sun is at its hottest—presumably the time when their god is at his zenith—Elijah goes a step further: "At noon Elijah began to taunt them. 'Shout louder!' he said. 'Surely he is a god! Perhaps he is deep in thought, or busy, or traveling. Maybe he is sleeping and must be awakened'" (1 Kings 18:27). The prophet must have had an incredibly sarcastic sense of humor, and this was doubtless the most enjoyable moment of the experience. He mocks Baal. If he were truly a god, then surely he could hear his people. Maybe the batteries in his hearing aid are dead! Perhaps he took an extra sleeping pill! There must be some explanation for why Baal doesn't answer! "So they shouted louder and slashed themselves with swords and spears, as was their custom, until their blood flowed" (18:28).

You know, if sincerity could save, these people surely would have been saved. They were the most sincere people in the world—but they were sincerely wrong. They had the wrong object for their faith. And faith is always determined by its object. In the midst of confrontation, in what do you place your faith? Elijah had faith in God—strong faith that allowed him to face down the lies of idolatry.

Is the object of your faith to be trusted? Let me illustrate. Suppose you were waiting for a plane that happens to be seriously delayed. While you are sitting there fuming, you are approached by a stranger. "Hey, friend," he says to you, "you really look like you need to get somewhere pretty badly. I'm leaving in a few minutes. I have my own private plane. Would you like to catch a ride?"

You think, why not? So you follow this man out onto the tarmac, and he leads you to an ancient prop plane held together with chewing gum and baling wire. I mean, this thing looks like it's been through *both* world wars! It only has half a prop. Part of the tail assembly is missing. "Wait a second," you say, thinking over the situation. "Just how safe is this thing?"

"I really don't know," comes the fellow's cheery reply. "Actually, I've never flown in it before. But I'm fascinated with the concept of flying. So let's try it out! I know, I know, it looks a little weathered, but. . . come on, have a little faith. Hop in!"

Would you? No way! Getting into that plane would not be an act of faith—it would be an act of foolishness. Why? Because the object of that pilot's faith is worthless. It doesn't matter what his intentions are or how great his sincerity happens to be. That plane is a piece of junk.

The same principle applies for Christians in confrontation. It is not sincerity that counts—neither ours nor our opponent's. What matters is the truth of what we believe. And we believe in the one true God. That's the solid foundation on which our faith is based. So no matter how sincerely others believe their man-made philosophies, our anchor is an abiding, eternal truth.

4. Openness

After the utter failure of the priests of Baal to coax their god into action, it becomes Elijah's turn to reveal the true God. "Then Elijah said to all the people, 'Come here to me'" (18:30). This command might seem like a small thing, but it reveals a key principle in confrontation: do things openly.

One of the hallmarks of the cults is that they have secret signs, secret words, secret practices, and so on. Many groups set up some sort of hierarchy, where only the privileged few at the top are privy to the "deeper truths." But Christians are to do everything in the open. Scripture doesn't call for any secret practices. When we join the church, we don't learn any secret handshakes or hidden truths. If we want to learn the deep truths of the faith, all we have to do is read the Bible. If we want to experience intimacy with God, we have only to spend time in prayer and fasting. There aren't any "secrets" to life in Christ. That is one of the unique characteristics of Christianity. It isn't a religion; it's a relationship with God.

I appreciate the biblical author noting how Elijah called the people to crowd in around him. "Get closer," he was saying. "You don't want to miss this." The Prophet wanted everyone to *see* what was about to happen. He didn't want anyone going away wondering, "Did he do some sort of trick?" He wanted everything to be clear, so that God would have the glory.

Jesus said something similar when the soldiers came to arrest him. He asked, "Am I leading a rebellion that you have come out with swords and clubs to capture me? Every day I was with you, teaching in the temple courts, and you did not arrest me" (Mark 14:48–49). His point was that He had performed His ministry in public, where everyone could judge it. By contrast, the priests and Sadducees had to arrest Him in secret, for fear of what people might say.

God wants your life be so transparent that people know who you are and what you stand for. Obviously there are certain societies and situations where Christians must operate in secret. But that is almost never the case in the United States. Therefore, when you have to take a stand for the Lord, don't hide it. Don't act as though you have to be afraid that someone might find out you are a believer. Let your battles be fought openly and boldly, so that no one can later accuse you of manipulation.

5. Boldness

After gathering the people around him, Elijah started giving orders. First he had someone from each tribe of Israel help him build an altar to God. Next he arranged the wood, cut the sacrificial bull into pieces, and then laid them on the altar. The sacrifice was ready—almost.

"Fill four large jars with water and pour it on the offering and on the wood," the prophet commanded (1 Kings 18:33). Can you imagine that? In the first place, there had now been a drought for three years, so water wasn't exactly easy to come by. In fact, the closest source was probably the Mediterranean Sea. So the people had to hike down the mountain to fill the jars with sea water, then hike back up and pour the water on the altar.

"Do it again," Elijah said when they were finished (18:34). So back down they went. A little while later they came panting back up, and doused the altar again.

"Do it a third time," the prophet commanded (18:34), and by now they were beginning to catch on. It was not just the bitter irony of thirsty, exhausted people hauling twelve jars of undrinkable water that Elijah was orchestrating. He had a practical end in view: he wanted that altar and its contents utterly saturated, so that no fire of human origin could light it. No tricks! It would take a miracle to burn this baby—a miracle from a God of fire!

One has to appreciate Elijah's boldness. He was trusting God for a mighty big miracle. How often do we do that? For example, I know parents who pray with their kids only about the small things: give us a safe trip, help Junior to get over his cold, help us to get a good night's sleep. But they stop short of asking God to do something great. Please understand, I'm not saying that anyone should stop praying for the little things; on the contrary, Scripture says to bring all things before the Lord. But I wonder, what will build the faith of our children faster—praying for things we know will probably happen anyway, or praying for God to do something truly miraculous?

Frankly, I think some of us as parents are afraid to pray boldly with our kids. We worry, "What's going to happen to their faith if God doesn't answer our prayers?" I don't know, but I do know what will happen to their faith if their view of God is too small. I mean, if we don't have enough faith to trust God for that which is genuinely difficult and impossible, why give our lives to Him in the first place? Why bother to worship God if we see Him as powerless, a God who can't really intervene in this life?

I once read a true story of a college freshman who had his Christian convictions confronted head-on by a physics professor. On the first day of class, the professor said, "Some of you have brought some quaint old notions of God and the supernatural to school with you. Well, let me put that out of your head right now." Then, as he held up a piece of chalk, he said, "Physics tells us that if I drop this piece of chalk on the floor, it will break. All of your praying to some alleged God can do nothing to stop it." Then he dropped the chalk, and it shattered into a hundred tiny fragments. Pretty convincing stuff, right?

Well, every week for an entire semester, the professor continued to challenge the students with his chalk. Finally, on the last day of class, he asked them, "Have I convinced you? Or does someone still retain their tired old notion of a God that is greater than science?"

The young man raised his hand. "I do, sir," he stated boldly. All semester, while he was learning the rudiments of physical science, this fellow had been preparing for this day. He knew it was coming, and he had asked several Christian friends to pray for him in what he was about to do.

"Well," the professor replied with amused surprise, "and do you think all your praying is going to stop my chalk from breaking as I drop it on the floor?"

"Yes sir, I do," he said, and he started to pray. Out loud! In class! "Lord, reveal yourself to these people. Don't let the chalk break today when it is dropped on the floor."

As you might guess, this completely set the professor off. He lost all sense of amusement and began railing at the student, insisting he "stop this nonsense." Then suddenly, in the midst of his tirade, he flung up his hands. The chalk, which he had been grasping tightly, slipped out, flew up in the air, dropped onto the cuff of the professor's pants, dropped down onto his shoe, and gently rolled onto the floor—unbroken!

The class burst into laughter, and then applause. The professor, utterly flummoxed, began spouting how "that meant nothing!" But the Christian simply smiled. God had answered his prayer in a public way, and everybody knew it.

Don't you just love the boldness of that student? Please don't misunderstand, I'm not suggesting that you put God in a box by telling the Almighty what He has to do. God is not your personal genie. Realize that this student's bold public prayer grew out of a discipline of private prayer and unqualified obedience to the Lord.

Do you ever tire of praying for "the same old stuff"? If so, then consider whether you believe we have a God who raises the dead, heals the sick, and creates something out of nothing? That's the God who wants to work miraculously through you in the midst of confrontation. That's the God of Elijah, and his faith in that God gave him boldness— so much that he even put "obstacles" in the way—just to make it memorable!

6. Prayer

We've seen a great deal of prayer already in Elijah's life. Now, as the contest with Baal draws to its climax, this great leader prays once more: "O Lord, God of Abraham, Isaac, and Israel. . . Let it be known today that you are God in Israel and that I am your servant and have done all these things at your command. Answer me, O Lord. . .so these people will know that you, O Lord, are God, and that you are turning their hearts back again" (18:36–37).

Please observe the content of the prophet's prayer. He asked that the people would be convinced of the reality of Jehovah, and that they would recognize that Elijah was merely His representative. Simple, brief, and to the point—quite a contrast to the labored prayers of the false prophets that lasted more than six hours.

Elijah's example suggests that when we are in the midst of a spiritual battle, we need to keep in constant communication with God. Paul tells us the same thing when he describes our spiritual armor in Ephesians 6. He reminds us to "pray in the Spirit on all occasions with all kinds of prayers and requests" (Ephesians 6:18). He knew the importance of relying on the Lord when faced with confrontation.

What was the result of Elijah's prayer? "Then the fire of the Lord fell and burned up the sacrifice, the wood, the stones and the soil, and also licked up the water in the trench" (1 Kings 18:38). Wow! That's what the people felt when they saw this demonstration of power from the one true God. They were in awe. They "fell prostrate and cried, 'The Lord—He is God! The Lord—He is God!'" (18:39).

What an unexpected transformation! In the morning, Baal worship prevailed. At the end of the day, worship of the Lord was back in style—thanks to the bold prayers of one faithful man.

7. Victory

All that remained was to clean up. The sacrifice was gone. In fact, so was the altar! So the only garbage left were the false prophets. Elijah gave instructions concerning them: "'Seize the prophets of Baal. Don't let anyone get away!' They seized them, and Elijah had them brought down to the Kishon Valley and slaughtered there" (18:40).

Does this seem a bit extreme? Not according to the Law. The penalty for false prophets was death (Deuteronomy 13:1–5). God knew that when there was a malignancy in the nation, it would have to be thoroughly excised before there could be any lasting victory. Thus Elijah was acting as a spiritual surgeon, knowing he had to hurt in order to heal. I think sometimes we moderns sit in judgment on the Old Testament without taking into account the tragic effects of sin that is not judged with severity.

At the same time, we can thank God that we live in a day of grace. He still judges sin, but His ultimate judgment of sin took place on the cross, where Jesus paid the penalty. He died the death. He took the judgment. Therefore, even false prophets can now find forgiveness and redemption—provided they repent of their sin and renounce their unbelief and rebellion.

As we come to the close of this dramatic portion of God's Word, let me suggest three principles that answer our question, what kind of person does God choose and use?

First, God uses a person who is convinced that God-plus-one equals a majority. Divine mathematics is vastly different from human mathematics. We may be impressed by numbers; God is not. Eight-hundred-fifty to one? No problem! In the divine calculus, it is eight-hundred-fifty to *one-plus-God*. The significance is not the one, but the God who empowers the one.

I love to study the gospels to see how God launched the church. He could have used any number of means, but He chose one method that establishes a pattern for us. Jesus Christ's focus was not on the multitudes—who followed him largely for superficial reasons—but on a small band of people into whose lives he built His character. When we come to the book of Acts, we read that these people "turned the world upside down" (Acts 17:6). In fact, the early church, which started with a mere handful of believers, may have been closer to winning its world for the gospel than we are with all of our technological advances and financial resources.

In the spiritual world, it is never "how many," it is always "what kind?" The question is not "what can we do?" but "what can God do?" Don't be overwhelmed by the size of the enemy, be confident in the size of your God.

A second principle is that God uses people who are potential-oriented, not problem oriented. Elijah could have wrung his hands and said, "So many oppose me! What can I do?" Instead, he allowed God to do a great work.

Numbers 13 records that the children of Israel, wending their way through the wilderness, made a crucial decision at Kedesh Barnea that determined their destiny. God had told them to go directly into the land. Instead, they decided to create a committee. In typical fashion, the committee came back with minority and majority reports. Caleb gave the minority report: "We should go up and take possession of the land, for we can certainly do it" (Numbers 13:30). Caleb believed the people were able because *God was able.* But the majority report was different: "We can't attack those people; they are stronger than we are . . .The land we explored devours those living in it. All the people we saw are of great size" (13:31–33).

Today, almost any Sunday School student can tell you the names of Caleb and Joshua, but can anyone think of who the ten men were who brought the majority report? Their names are given at the start of that chapter. But who wants to remember them? They were a bunch of problem-oriented guys who looked around and saw obstacles everywhere. Joshua and Caleb saw the giants, too. But they saw the potential of victory because the great God of the universe had commanded them to go up and take the territory. God used Joshua and Caleb. The other ten became forgotten figures of history.

Finally, God uses people who focus not so much on their ability as on their availability. You may feel that you can't do very much, that you don't have much ability or opportunity. But you can do all that God wants you to do. If you focus on your abilities, you become proud and God cannot use you. If you focus on your lack of abilities, you become negative and God will not use you. First Corinthians 4:2 tells us that "it is required that those who have been given a trust must prove faithful." The passage is talking about us as believers. We don't have to prove ourselves brilliant, or gifted, or spectacular. Just faithful.

The more I study the life of Elijah, the more I realize that what James said of him was true: He was a man just like us (James 5:17). An ordinary man who lived an extraordinary life. That's Elijah's claim to fame.

I remember watching a particular student one day and wondering, "Lord, what in the world are you going to do with this guy? How is he ever going to make it? He's got nothing going for him!" When he graduated, he accepted the pastorate of a tiny, dying church in Canada. Nineteen men had walked away from that pulpit. The congregation's spiritual life was in shambles. So I figured, "This guy must be too dumb to turn it down!"

Well, guess who was dumb? Years later, I was still hearing about that fellow. He had taken that broken-down church and set it on fire for the Lord. People were growing. Unbelievers were getting saved left and right. The board had launched a building campaign—the first one in 123 years!

Meanwhile, there was another student who passed through the seminary. He had every gift a pastor could want: charisma, warmth, an incredible ability to communicate effectively. I was convinced that this man had a bright future. But after graduating, he split a church and then divorced his wife to take up with another woman. Today, he's out of the ministry completely (thank heaven).

The lesson of these two men is that brilliance is sterile unless it is coupled with commitment. God may prefer a sharp tool to a dull one, but He'll use the dull one if that's all that is available. Elijah was simply a man who made himself available for God. When a confrontation arose, he was willing to take a stand for God and use his gifts as best he could for the Lord's purposes. Could God use you in a similar way in your world?

CHAPTER FOUR

Communication

If you were asked to choose a pattern for your prayer life, it is unlikely that you would select Elijah. "After all," you might argue, "Elijah was a mighty prophet of God. I'm not. Elijah was a worker of miracles. I most certainly am not." Somehow we have managed to wrap Elijah in a mantle of supernaturalism, with the result that he appears remote and unapproachable.

But that isn't how James describes him. Remember what he said? "Elijah was a man just like us" (James 5:17). To appreciate that comment, let me remind you of two things concerning James. First, his epistle has more to say about the doctrine of prayer than any other book in the New Testament. It is full of instruction on praying. Second, tradition holds that James was nicknamed Camel Knees by the early church, so calloused were his knees from incessant kneeling to pray. I like that! When the Holy Spirit wants to teach us about prayer, He selects a practitioner, not a theorist. Doctrine is dynamic. Truth is designed not to satisfy our curiosity, but to overhaul our experience.

So what motivated Camel Knees? What turned him on to prayer? Who was his pattern? His letter mentions Elijah—a man "just like us." The Bible does not say, "Elijah was a mighty prophet of God who prayed," nor, "Elijah was a miracle worker who prayed." It says he was a man *just like us*. Cut from the same bolt of human cloth. He had problems and perplexities, doubts and disappointments, fears and frustrations. But he prayed. That's really what made him different. And that's why James selected him as his paragon of prayer. Scripture is telling us that if Elijah could be like us in our passions, we can be like him in our prayer.

A careful look at 1 Kings 18 reveals the prophet Elijah in this kind of communication with God. This is certainly not the first time we have read of his prayer life. Earlier we saw that Elijah prayed that it might not rain (1 Kings 17:1; James 5:17). Prayer also preceded a later encounter with King Ahab (1 Kings 18:16). And Mount Carmel, it was prayer that brought down the fire (18:36–37). Now Elijah is going to pray for a flood.

Keep in mind that God had already promised that it was going to rain: "After a long time, in the third year, the word of the Lord came to Elijah, 'Go and present yourself to Ahab, and I will send rain on the land'" (18:1). If God had already promised rain, then why pray for it? Because prayer is the hand of faith that translates promise into performance. God not only ordains the end, he also ordains the means. Prayer is not a question of coming to a reluctant God in an attempt to persuade Him to do what He really does not want to do. Prayer is a matter of coming before God with an awareness that we are dependent individuals. It is the realization that our need is not partial, but total.

Shortly after I became a Christian, someone wrote in the flyleaf of my Bible this couplet: "When I try, I fail. When I trust, He succeeds." There is a world of theology in those two lines. The Christian life is not a life of trying, it is a life of trusting. It is a recognition that living according to godliness is not difficult, it's impossible, because it requires a super-natural invasion.

The Earnestness of Prayer

There are three characteristics of Elijah's prayer life that I trust the Spirit of God will weave into the fabric of our experience. First, note the earnestness of Elijah's prayer.

Near the end of 1 Kings 18, we read, "And Elijah said to Ahab, 'Go, eat and drink, for there is the sound of a heavy rain'" (18:41). We discover in a subsequent verse that there were no clouds in the sky, so how could the prophet have heard the sound of a heavy rain? The answer lies in the fact that Elijah was in close, constant communication with God. The Lord had already promised the rain, so Elijah knew it was com-ing. Even though he couldn't see a cloud, he could hear it with the ears of faith.

Have you ever been that certain of anything? Has God ever made something so clear to you that you just believed it, regardless of the present circumstances? Elijah had that confidence.

King Ahab, meanwhile, was not nearly as impressed. I find that hard to believe, considering what he had just witnessed. But instead of falling on his face in repentance, Ahab went off to have dinner. Elijah, by contrast, "climbed up to the top of Carmel, bent down to the ground and put his face between his knees" (18:42). The text mentions this posture, not because it is a pattern for prayer, but because the prophet's outward demeanor gave evidence of his inward earnestness.

Remember our Lord in the Garden of Gethsemane? He prostrat-ed Himself on the ground as He cried out, "If it is possible, may this cup be taken from me. Yet not as I will, but as you will" (Matthew 26:39). His physical position was a reflection of the spiritual attitude in His heart.

James tells us that Elijah "prayed earnestly," a phrase that literally translates, "He prayed in his prayer." Isn't that a great thought? Elijah was so caught up in his communication with the Almighty that he just said whatever was in his heart. He talked with God as though He were physically right there with him. That's earnestness.

Have you ever had the opportunity to listen to a new convert pray? It is so refreshing! One time we led a man to Christ through our home Bible class ministry. He came to know the Lord on a Thursday evening, and on Sunday he showed up at church. The pastor announced that we were going to have an evening service, and of course the guy didn't know enough to stay home. So he showed up again. That's when he learned that our church had a Bible study and prayer meeting on Wednesday night, so he came that evening as well.

I sat next to him at the prayer meeting, and just before we got started, he turned to me and asked, "Do you think they'd mind if I prayed?"

"Of course not," I reassured him. "That's what we're here for."

"Yeah, I know," he said, "But I've got a problem. I can't pray the way you people do."

I told him, "That's no problem, friend. You should thank God for that!"

Well, we started praying, and I could tell he was too nervous to take part. Finally I put my hand on his thigh to encourage him. I'll never forget his prayer: "Lord, this is Jim," he began. "I'm the one who met you last Thursday night? I'm sorry, Lord, because I can't say it the way the rest of these people do, but I want to tell you the best I know how. I love you, Lord. I really do. Thanks a lot. I'll see you later."

I tell you, that prayer ignited our prayer meeting! Some of us had been doing a good job of talking about theology in prayer—you know, exploring the universe of doctrine, scraping the Milky Way with our big words. But this guy prayed—earnestly!

My children have taught me many things about theology. When they were quite young, we had a scholar visiting our home. After our meal, we were ready for our customary time of family worship, and we invited the man to join us. When it came time to pray, the kids, in typical childlike fashion, thanked Jesus for the tricycle and the sandbox and the fence and so on. Our guest could scarcely wait to take me aside.

"Professor Hendricks," he began, very much the lecturer that he was, "you don't mean to tell me that you're a professor in a theological seminary, and yet you teach your children to pray for things like that?"

"I certainly do," I replied. "Do you ever pray about your Ford?" I knew he did. He had to: he was riding mostly on faith and frayed fabric!

"Of course," he replied, "but that's different."

"Oh, really?" I countered. "What makes you think your Ford is more important to God than my boy's tricycle?" Then I pressed him further. "You're on the road a lot. Do you ever pray for protection?"

"Brother Hendricks, I never go anywhere but that I pray for the Lord's journeying mercies."

"Well, safety is essentially what my boy is thanking Jesus for when he thanks him for the fence. That fence keeps out those great big dogs on the other side!"

I'm afraid that this man had the same problem as many of us. We are educated beyond our intelligence. It's refreshing to have a new convert move into our midst, or a child who in simplicity and earnestness of heart just talks to God. God delights in the honesty of a believing heart.

When Elijah kneeled down up on top of Mount Carmel, he poured out his heart, earnestly praying for what was most on his mind—water. Many of us who are Christians need to drop the clichés and fancy words, and focus instead on developing an earnest heart before our Lord.

The Expectation of Prayer

The second characteristic of Elijah's prayer life was the expectation of his prayer. Three statements in three verses of 1 Kings 18 reveal the story of an answer to prayer: "There is nothing there" (18:43); "A cloud as small as a man's hand is rising" (18:44); and "A heavy rain came on" (18:45). From nothing, to a small cloud, to a heavy rain—that's the progression of God's answer.

The thing for us to notice is that Elijah prayed expectantly: "'Go and look toward the sea,' he told his servant. And he went up and looked. 'There is nothing there,' he said. Seven times Elijah said, 'Go back.' The seventh time the servant reported, 'A cloud as small as a man's hand is rising from the sea.' So Elijah said, 'Go and tell Ahab, "Hitch up your chariot and go down before the rain stops you.'"" (18:43–44).

Seven times! I think most of us would have thrown in the towel long before that. And I wonder, what if Elijah had stopped on the sixth time? You see, in expectant faith, the prophet sends his servant to scan the skies because he is looking for something. He keeps sending the man back because he expects God to answer. If we expect nothing, we will seldom be disappointed.

There is a great example of this principle in Acts 12. The account says that "Peter was kept in prison, but the church was earnestly praying to God for him" (Acts 12:5). So God answered their prayers and miraculously released Peter from prison. Finding himself free, the apostle "went to the house of Mary the mother of John, also called Mark, where many people had gathered and were praying" (12:12). What were they praying for? For Peter's deliverance, of course. "Peter knocked at the outer entrance, and a servant girl named Rhoda came to answer the door. When she recognized Peter's voice, she was so overjoyed she ran back without opening it and exclaimed, 'Peter is at the door!'" (12:13–14).

Do you get the picture? This little gal looks through the peephole and says, "Good grief! It's Peter!" She's so excited, she forgets to let him in. She runs back to tell the others, "Hey! Peter's out there." And did they stand to sing the Hallelujah Chorus? No! They said to her, "You're out of your mind" (12:15).

"Look," the girl insists, "it's Peter. I saw him."

"It can't be Peter. He's in jail. You must be seeing things."

Rhoda wouldn't be quiet though, so eventually some astute soul in the crowd came up with a more profound theological answer: "Well, then it must be Peter's angel" (12:15). Problem is, they weren't praying for his angel to be delivered; they were praying for Peter himself to be delivered. Fortunately, the answer to their prayer kept knocking—and since it was Peter, probably knocking pretty loudly about this time! So when someone finally wised up and opened the door, "they were astonished," it says (12:16). Knocked out, is more like it. God had actually answered their prayers!

Now before you jump all over these early Christians, remember that you may have had a similar response. Suppose somebody came up to you and said, "Hey, you know your brother whom you've been praying for for the last twenty-two years?"

"You mean Bill? Yeah, he's been a great burden on my heart. He's a total reprobate. The entire family is ashamed of him."

"Well, guess what, you got an answer."

"What?"

"The Lord has answered your prayer."

"You've got to be kidding!."

"Really! Bill went forward at an altar call last week and trusted Christ as his Savior."

"Are you sure it was Bill?"

"Absolutely! I was there. He was saved."

"No, you must have seen somebody else. Bill would never accept Christ."

This is where we need to develop Elijah-like faith. May his tribe increase! He said, "God told me it would rain. Okay, I can hear it coming. Go look for it." Somebody says to him, "No, nothing there." And what is his response? "Look again. It's coming." And eventually the rains came. Don't you enjoy being with positive people? It's a blessing to spend time with a person whose belief in God's promises is so solid that he anticipates the Lord's work?

We used to have a family in our community who had that sort of confidence in God. The father decided that the Lord wanted him in vocational Christian work, so he sold his business and entered the ministry. Things got rather tough financially, and one night at family devotions, Timmy, the youngest of four boys, said, "Daddy, do you think Jesus would mind if I asked Him for a shirt?"

"Of course not," his dad answered.

Now this family used a tool that I would strongly recommend to every parent. They had a little notebook, and on one side of a page they wrote, "We Ask," and on the other side, "He Answers." So in response to Timmy's request, they wrote, "Shirt for Timmy." Mom even added the words, "Size seven."

You can be sure that every night after that, Timmy saw to it that they prayed for his shirt. They prayed for weeks. Then one day, the mother received a telephone call from a clothier in downtown Dallas who happened to be a Christian. "I just completed our July clearance sale," he told her. "Knowing that you have four boys, it occurred to me that I have something you might use. Would you like some boys' shirts?"

"What size?" the mother asked.

"Seven," the retailer replied.

"How many do you have?"

"Twelve of them."

What would you do? This mom, praising God all the way, went and picked up the shirts. But she didn't just stuff them in Timmy's bureau drawer and make some casual comment about it later. No, that night, when Timmy said, "Let's pray for the shirt," his mother interrupted.

"We don't have to pray for the shirt, Timmy. The Lord has answered your prayer."

"He did?" the little boy asked with amazement.

"Right." And, by prior arrangement, one of Timmy's older brothers went out, got a shirt, brought it in, and put it on the table in front of Timmy. His eyes were big as saucers. Then another of the boys went out, got another shirt, and laid that one in front of Timmy. Out and back, out and back, until Timmy had twelve shirts on the table, and he's thinking that maybe God has gone into the shirt business.

Today, Timmy is a man in Dallas who understands that God in heaven, immense as He is, is still interested in a little boy's need for a new shirt. Ask yourself: Do your kids know that? As you raise them in an affluent society, do you help them develop trust in the Lord by encouraging the expectancy of waiting on God, even for the little things?

Elijah had that. God sent birds to feed him every day (1 Kings 17:4, 6). Consequently, he understood the importance of waiting with expectation before the Lord.

Not that God answers every prayer. Sometimes we have to write "No" in the answer column. That, too, is part of His communication with us. It is just as much an answer as a yes. My wife and I prayed for two additional children for our family. Twice God appeared to be answering that prayer—but twice we were given miscarriages. I can remember coming home from the hospital and meeting my four kids at the door, asking, "Hey Dad! Is it a boy or a girl?" And I had to take them over to the sofa and tell them that God's answer was no. You communicate more in one experience like that than in two dozen sermons on the subject of prayer. It comes through at a level a child can understand. The problem, though, is that often we adults don't get the message.

Trusting God may lead to a yes or no, but most of the time our expectancy must be demonstrated by waiting. Some answers to our family's prayer list were a long time in coming. One of them was the salvation of my father, a retired military officer. Shortly before his retirement, he flew down to Dallas to see us, and of course my kids were all excited. "Grand-daddy's coming! Grand-daddy's coming! I hope he'll wear his uniform."

When my dad appeared in the doorway of the plane, in uniform, with all his ribbons displayed across his chest, our youngest boy Bill took off to meet him. Those were the days when you de-planed down stairs onto the tarmac, and when Dad got to the bottom of the ramp, Bill threw his arms around him. Just as I caught up with them, I heard him ask, "Hey, Grand-daddy, do you know Jesus yet?"

My father looked a bit flustered; he certainly hadn't expected that question! Finally he replied, "No, son, I...I'm afraid I can't say I do."

"Well, you will pretty soon," Bill replied, "cause we're prayin' for you!"

"Pretty soon" turned into many years. In fact, Dad didn't turn his life over to Christ until four months prior to his death in 1974. I had personally prayed for him for forty-two years.

Maybe you've been praying for something or someone for a long time. It might be the salvation of a loved one, or a change in a country, or the success of a ministry. I want to encourage you, on the authority of the Word of God, to go to the brow of the hill again and look with expectation. The Savior said, "*Keep on* asking and you will receive. *Keep on* seeking and you will find. *Keep on* knocking and it will be opened to you" (Matthew 7:7). Ask, seek, and knock with expectancy. God is still at work answering prayers.

The Effect of Prayer

Be sure you don't miss the third characteristic of Elijah's prayer life—the effect of his prayer. Returning to the top of Mount Carmel, "The sky grew black with clouds, the wind rose, a heavy rain came on. . . ." (1 Kings 18:45). There is a twofold effect described in this passage. First, there was the effect upon the land. The rainshower that fell was no light drizzle. It was no soft, summer sprinkle, enough to moisten the land but not to satisfy the drought. This was a heavy, soaking down-pour that broke the prolonged dry spell.

Today we live in a spiritually arid culture. Many people feel sur-rounded by a spiritual desert. I believe God is looking for people who can call down the refreshing rains of His grace that will break people's spiritu-al drought.

The second effect of Elijah's prayer was a great effect upon the man. "The power of the Lord came upon Elijah and, tucking his cloak into his belt, he ran ahead of Ahab all the way to Jezreel" (18:46). Just as the land was renewed, Elijah himself emerged from the experience with a new dynamic. The power of God came upon him. There was no greater testimony than that. It came because Elijah knew how to lay hold of the throne of God in prayer.

This is a valuable principle to keep in mind: great praying brings great blessing. Elijah's prayer wasn't great because of its language, or its length, or its loudness. It was great because it was earnest, it was expec-tant, and it was invested in the living God.

However, it was also dangerous to pray that way. Elijah learned that lesson. He had prayed that it would not rain, and the answer to his prayer was a drying brook. Now he prayed that it would rain, and the answer was a deluge. Great praying brings great blessing.

When I was a boy, I was privileged to sit under the ministry of Dr. L.L. Legters, a great Bible teacher of another generation. He recounted once occasion when he was pastor of a church. He was walking down the street with fifty dollars in his pocket, and a missionary home on furlough met him.

"Dr. Legters," the missionary said, "I think it's providential that we've met. We're having an urgent prayer meeting at the church. We'd love to have you join us."

"Well," said Dr. Legters, who was sort of a brusque individual, "Let's not pray out of ignorance. Let's pray out of intelligence. Exactly what is it that you need?"

"We have an urgent financial need. We need fifty dollars."

So they went to the prayer meeting, went around the circle, and everybody prayed. But at the end of the time, one of those gathered commented, "I don't feel that we've really laid hold of the Lord in this."

"Then let's pray some more," someone suggested. So they went around the circle a second time. Then a third time. It was then that Dr. Legters felt God saying to him, "Legters, what about that fifty dollars in your pocket?"

Never one to delay the inevitable, the pastor interrupted a woman right in the middle of her prayer. "Hold it!" he said, and reached into his pocket. "God just answered your prayer," he said, placing the money on the table.

I can still remember him telling that story, years after it happened, then pointing a long, bony finger at us and saying, "Ladies and gentlemen, it's a dangerous thing to pray!"

It still is. Don't ever pray unless you want to get involved. Don't ever pray unless you are personally committed, because the answer to your prayer may start with you.

James warns us, "You do not have because you do not ask; you do not receive because you ask with wrong motives, that you may spend what you get on your pleasures" (James 4:2–3). For several years, I have been asking myself why the one area in my Christian life in which I constantly bomb out is my prayer life. It's not an accident, either. It's the result of cultivation.

The older I get, the more impressed I am with the subtlety of Satan. He always fogs us out in the crucial areas, never the trivial. Satan does not mind us witnessing, as long as we don't pray. He knows that it is far more important that we talk with God about men than that we talk with men about God. He doesn't really mind if we study the Bible, just as long as we don't pray. He knows that apart from talking with the God who gave us His Word, the Word will never get into our life. We will simply develop a severe case of spiritual pride—and Satan loves that. He doesn't mind our becoming compulsively active in our local church or in some other form of Christian work—sometimes I think he encourages it—just so long as we do not pray. That way, we will be active, but not accomplish anything.

The gospels record only fifty-two days in the life of our Lord. Mark 1 tells of one of his busiest. It was a day crowded with miracles, teaching, and healing. Only a person who has sustained a public ministry has any idea of the physical, emotional, and spiritual drain of constant interaction with people.

Notice what our Lord did: "Very early in the morning, while it was still dark, Jesus got up, left the house and went off to a solitary place, where he prayed" (Mark 1:35). Now if Jesus Christ, who had unbroken communication with the Father, needed to pray, what must my need be? What must yours be? So high on his priority list was communication with the infinite God that after a busy day of service, he got up long before sunrise and went to a solitary place to pray.

I believe the work of God is languishing in many areas, not for lack of divine power, but for lack of human prayer. We fight, we scheme, we toil, we do everything we can—except pray. But, as James says, we have not because we ask not.

Elijah asked. He stayed in constant communication with the Lord by praying earnestly and expectantly. As a result, he saw the effect of his prayer. You, too, can see the power of God change your world by learning to pray. That's what turns loose His power!

CHAPTER FIVE

Commitment

My father was a career Army man whose later years were spent at the Pentagon in Washington, D.C. One time while I was visiting him there, I came across a fascinating reprint of an article by Gen. Douglas MacArthur, the lionhearted leader of America's Asian forces in World War II. The article, entitled "Requisites for Military Success," cited four principles that the general deemed most important.

First, there must be *morale*. A fighting force must be united by an esprit de corps, a will to win, and the sense of a cause worth dying for. Second, there must be *strength*. The military must have adequately trained and well-equipped personnel to do its job. Third, there must be an *adequate source of supply*. Lifelines must be kept open so that those at the front receive all that they need to win.

The bulk of the article, though, was devoted to the fourth principle.

In order to prevail, an army must have a *knowledge of the enemy*. MacArthur wrote, "The greater the knowledge of the enemy, the greater the potential of victory." He traced this principle through military history, beginning with Joshua in the Old Testament and ending with the North Africa campaign of the Second World War.

Knowing the enemy has its parallel in the spiritual realm. Paul recognized that, for he told the Corinthians that he did not want Satan to gain an advantage over them. "For we are not unaware of his schemes" he wrote (2 Corinthians 2:11). That's true. We are not in the dark as to how our enemy operates. God has exposed his strategies in Scripture. Therefore, the greater our knowledge of our foe, the greater our potential for spiritual victory.

In 1 Kings 19, we find a case study in the strategy of Satan. The theme of this chapter could be summarized as, "Victory always makes us vulnerable." There is something about winning that elates us, takes us off guard, and thereby leaves us wide open to the devastating arrows of the evil one. This chapter reminds us that there is really but a short distance from the top of Mount Carmel to the bottom of the valley of despair. As believers, the only thing that rescues us from these low times is our commitment to the Lord.

In reading this record of Elijah's rout, the thing I appreciate the most is its realism. It is confirming proof of the inspiration of Scripture. When God paints a picture of a man, he paints him warts and all. He tells the story as it is, not glossed over like a cheap novel. From the standpoint of literary narrative, it would have been much more inspiring to have ended the account of Elijah's life with the great victory on Carmel (1 Kings 18:16–46). But that would have created a fable, not a record that is true to the facts.

The truth about Elijah—recalling James' words once more—is that he was "a man just like us" (James 5:17). And as a man, Elijah was prone to failure. Paul reminds us of this natural human tendency: "If you think you are standing firm, be careful that you don't fall!"

(1 Corinthians 10:12). His point is that we are susceptible to weakness at the very point we think we are strongest. Our moment of greatest triumph is the moment when we are most vulnerable.

1 Kings 18 and 19 bear this out. The two chapters stand in sharp contrast: a mountain-top experience followed by a black hole of despair. Somehow, the greatest victory in Elijah's life was immediately followed by his greatest defeat. We do well to take instruction from the prophet's downfall, because the devil is still employing the same devices today that he used on Elijah with such success thousands of years ago.

The Danger of Looking at Circumstances

Let's pick up the story at the tail end of 1 Kings 18. Roundly defeated and utterly disgusted, Ahab mounted his chariot and rode down from Mount Carmel to the plain of Esdraelon (1 Kings 18:45). It was about a thirty-five-mile trip to his home in Jezreel, so, needless to say, he got home rather late that night. He hoped that Jezebel had already gone to sleep. So he crept into the palace quietly, perhaps with his sandals in his hand.

But then he heard that all-too-familiar voice. "Ahab!"

"Uh, yes dear?" he replied glumly.

"You're not looking too good. What happened?"

"Look, Jez, I'm really tired. It's been a long day."

"Would you like something to eat?"

"No thanks. I lost my appetite."

"Well then, sit down, have a cup of coffee, and tell me what happened."

We can imagine that Ahab tried to change the subject ("Who do you think will win the Samaritan series?"), but his insistent wife kept pressing with her questions, trying to pry information out of her man. As a result, "Ahab told Jezebel everything Elijah had done and how he had killed all the prophets with the sword" (19:1).

The text tells us what happened next: "So Jezebel sent a messenger to Elijah to say, 'May the gods deal with me, be it ever so severely, if by this time tomorrow I do not make your life like that of one of them.' Elijah was afraid and ran for his life. When he came to Beersheba in Judah, he left his servant there" (19:2–3).

Up to this point, the only thing that has filled Elijah's vision is the Lord. But now, as if looking through the wrong end of a telescope and having his perception distorted, Elijah suddenly starts looking at his circumstances.

That is often the case for God's servants. Remember the time when Peter and the other disciples were out in a boat? They were doing a little night fishing, when all of a sudden they looked out over the starboard side and saw someone walking on the water. That scared them to death! But it was the Lord, and when He spoke, they recognized Him. Peter, in his characteristic fashion, said, "Lord, if it's you, tell me to come to you."

So the Lord said, "Come!" (Matthew 14:28–29).

Now that presented Peter with a problem. He had to step over the side and let go. I can just picture him gingerly taking his hands off the side of the boat—one at a time—and gingerly stepping across the water. Meanwhile, Philip and Andrew are bug-eyed in the back of the boat. However, as soon as Peter takes his eyes off the Lord Jesus and starts looking at his circumstances—the wind and the waves—he begins to sink. "What am I doing out here?" he suddenly asks himself. "I can't walk on water. I'm just a fisherman, for crying out loud!" That's when he starts to go under. And then—in what may be the most significant prayer in the New Testament; certainly it is the shortest—he cries out, "Lord, save me!" Jesus reaches down and rescues Peter from a watery grave (14:30–31).

Now how do you suppose Peter got back to the boat? The New Testament doesn't say anything about Christ carrying him back, so we can assume that he walked back. And I'm very confident that he kept his eyes on the Lord the whole time. The moment you and I begin to take our eyes off the source of our courage, we lose it. The moment we lose focus on the only One who can protect us and provide for us, we're going to start to slip.

That's why I admire Paul. In the book of Philippians, the apostle says, "Rejoice in the Lord always. I will say it again, Rejoice!" (Philippians 4:4). I used to read that verse and think, "My, what wonderful words!" Then I studied where Paul was when he wrote them. He wasn't in the Rome Ritz. He was under arrest! Yet he knew how to rejoice in the midst of reality. That kind of joy isn't just happiness, which comes from getting what you want. True joy is based on a complete trust in a loving God who has got a plan for your life.

Unfortunately, Elijah forgot that. After witnessing one of the greatest demonstrations of God's power recorded in Scripture, he took his eyes off of God and began looking at his circumstances. "Who am I to be taking on the king?" he suddenly asked himself. "How did I get myself in so deep? The queen is after me. I'd better get out of here!"

So he took off, and he didn't stop running until he was in Beersheba, 120 miles to the south. What he needed to do was keep his focus on the living Lord. That would have filled his mind with possibilities for what God could do, rather than the problem of what Jezebel had threatened to do. When one keeps his eyes on God, God becomes his chief commitment.

Don't fasten your eyes on circumstances; if you do, you're doomed to fall. If you keep your eyes on God, you allow Him to work through you. Remember, "Greater is He who is in you than he that is in the world" (1 John 4:4).

The Danger of Praying Foolishly

Elijah's reaction to Jezebel reveals a second danger to which we are constantly exposed: praying foolishly. Having put 120 miles between himself and the wicked queen, Elijah was still feeling the heat, so he "went a day's journey into the desert. He came to a broom tree, sat down under it and prayed that he might die. 'I have had enough, Lord,' he said. 'Take my life; I am no better than my ancestors'" (19:4).

That's an amazing passage of Scripture. One person threatens Elijah, and he's ready to turn in his prophet's badge! Despite having single-handedly taken on 850 prophets and prevailed, he now turns tail when faced with one vengeful woman!

As I read Elijah's prayer, I think I see a bit of the confusion he must have been feeling. Anytime you have a distorted perception of a situation, you become dishonest about it, even in your prayers. I don't think Elijah really wanted to die. If he wanted to die, he didn't have to travel 120 miles. All he had to do was make himself available to Jezebel. She would have been delighted to accommodate his request!

No, Elijah got caught up in seeing his situation incorrectly, which is to say that he forgot about his powerful God. As a result, he ended up praying for something he really didn't want because it seemed like the best solution to his problem. Again, he was so focused on his circumstances that he began lying to himself: "I've really blown it this time, Lord. I got Jezebel so mad at me that she wants to kill me. I guess I'm just no good."

Keep in mind what we said earlier about Elijah serving as our model for prayer. His throw-in-the-towel attitude doesn't take away from that. But it does show us that when we wallow in self-pity, our prayers can become pitiful. We forget about the good things that God has promised and performed, and our commitment to Him becomes muddled. Furthermore, like Elijah we start asking for things we don't really want.

Have you ever thanked the Lord for the blessing of unanswered prayer? I sometimes ponder the foolish things I've asked the Lord for, and I'm glad that He was smart enough not to grant them. Prayer is not asking for what *you* want; it is asking for what *God* wants.

One of the first verses of Scripture I ever memorized was Psalm 37:4: "Delight yourself in the Lord and He will give you the desires of your heart." I can still remember running that through my mind as a young person. "Wow! God will give me anything I ask for," I thought to myself. "What a deal!" But I discovered that I was usually delighting in *myself*, not in the Lord. My occupation was the desires of my heart, not the delights of my Lord. It has taken a lifetime, but as I've learned to delight myself in the Lord, I have found that He has changed my heart's desires to conform with His desires.

When I was a teenager, I courted a lovely young lady in Philadelphia. I lived in northeast Philadelphia ,and she lived in southwest Philadelphia. We could not have been further apart. It took me an hour and forty-five minutes to get from my house to hers. I had to take a trolley, a bus, a subway train, and another trolley. But I just had to see her! I can still remember dashing out the front door with my grandmother calling after me, "Howard, come back! You have to help with the dishes!"

"Sorry, Grandma," I'd yell from half-way down the block, "I can't. I gotta see my girl!"

And I'd go all the way across town to do what? Help her with dishes! To this day, I can't think of anything I found more delightful than doing dishes with the woman who eventually became my wife. Her delights were my desires.

That is exactly what happens in the spiritual realm. God's will becomes my will. His way becomes my way. His Word becomes my word. And when I am occupied with His delights, then by that strange spiritual metamorphosis, they become my desires. When I come to God in prayer, I need to say, "Lord, not what I want, but what you want." Even if it means death at the hand of Jezebel! Better to die in the will of God than to be comfortable and secure in a place outside of His will.

Elijah prayed foolishly. He anticipated the saying, "Be careful what you wish for; you may get it." Fortunately, we have a loving God who has patience with fools, and doesn't grant all of our foolish prayers.

The Danger of Neglecting Your Needs

Of all the traps that Satan uses to ensnare Christians today, perhaps none is more effective than self-neglect. We live in a high-pressure society, with demands coming at us from every angle. Faced with that onslaught, we have to realize that just because we happen to be a believer does not make us immune to having emotional and physical needs, just like any other human being.

Some time ago we had a very gifted student at Dallas Seminary who unfortunately lost his perspective in this area. He cut back on his sleep so as to study more and—as he perceived it—prepare himself for the Lord's work. He stopped doing anything recreational, because it interfered with his studies. He filled every waking moment with activity, never relaxing. He convinced himself that he was so committed to Christ that nothing, not even food or rest, should stand in his way. As a result, he never achieved a constructive ministry because he never took time to find out who he really was. He became a workaholic, trying to impress everybody with his achievements. But all he really did was alienate the people around him.

I once asked another student who was heading straight for burnout, "How come you don't smoke?"

He stared at me with one of those shocked looks and said, "Oh, Professor Hendricks, my body is the temple of the Holy Spirit! I could never destroy it with tobacco."

"Then why are you bent on destroying it with activity?" I asked him. "Why put your body in a premature grave by burning the candle at both ends—and all the way in between? Is that any way to honor God?"

Elijah fell into this same pitfall. He had been up long hours. He had been through an intensely stressful ordeal. The text tells us that he had run the thirty-five miles from Carmel to Jezreel ahead of Ahab's chariot (1 Kings 18:46)—an incredible marathon, even empowered as he was by the Lord. Then he ran another 120 miles to evade Jezebel's death warrant. Then he went a day's journey into the desert. No wonder he finally plopped down under the broom tree: he was ready to be swept up and thrown away!

No wonder, too, that he ended up saying and praying some very foolish things. Have you noticed that you sometimes make less than great decisions when you are overly fatigued or mentally drained? It's as if your brain has shut down, and you cannot think clearly. But if you were to take time to refresh yourself, your situation would appear entirely different, and your decision would reflect sound judgment.

Nevertheless, modern Christianity tends to make heroes out of leaders who burn themselves out. I don't know why that is. It's like a badge of honor to have pushed yourself to the wall so hard that you run into it. But—speaking from personal experience with this problem—I say that commitment to Christ is not a license to burn oneself out. Likewise, staying refreshed is no sign of a lack of commitment. We have gotten so busy that no one takes time to just stay at home and relax anymore. We rush around from one commitment to another, from meeting to meeting every night of the week. As a result, we constantly feel tired, our children feel they ought to be constantly entertained, and church somehow turns into a draining experience, a negative influence that pulls our families apart, rather than binding them together.

Elijah was there. He was worn, wearied, and wasted. Distressed, drooping, and dog-tired. Yet in the midst of that dismal scene, we are given a refreshing glimpse of the grace of God. Thoroughly spent, Elijah "lay down under the tree and fell asleep. All at once, an angel touched him and said, 'Get up and eat.' He looked around, and there by his head was a cake of bread baked over hot coals, and a jar of water. He ate and drank and then lay down again" (19:5–6).

Just think of it: God sent an angel on a mission of mercy to prepare a meal for His servant. The angel prepares the meal, awakens the prophet, Elijah eats, and then, from sheer exhaustion, he goes back to sleep again. "Then the angel of the Lord came back a second time and touched him and said, 'Get up and eat, for the journey is too much for you'" (19:7). God cares for the needs of His servants.

Of course, the journey Elijah had taken was a journey out of God's will. Fortunately, he wasn't out of God's concern. The Lord graciously, tenderly provided for Elijah's physical needs. That's because He wanted Elijah ready for the moment when God would reveal Himself.

Perhaps you can identify with Elijah. Perhaps you think it's better to burn out than to rust out. But that is utter nonsense. Elijah was never at risk of rusting out. And the question is not whether to burn out or rust out, but how can we live out our faith? The answer is, by relying on the wisdom and balance that come through the ministry of the Holy Spirit in our lives.

My friend David Roper has wisely pointed out that "it's good to know that our melancholy may be nothing but natural weariness. We're too inclined to make something profound or 'spiritual' out of it." I find this true in working with people. Someone will come to me for counsel about their irritability or sense of tension. "What you really need is a good night's sleep," I often tell them That may not sound very spiritual, but think about it. If you've ever awakened with a headache, you know how unspiritual you feel. I make it a practice never to make a critical decision when I am exhausted or have a headache. One good night's sleep can do an amazing work to restore my perspective. That is essentially what God told Elijah to do.

After he slept, he once more "got up and ate and drank. Strengthened by that food, he traveled forty days and forty nights until he reached Horeb, the mountain of God" (19:8). Horeb is another two hundred miles to the south, so Elijah ended up traveling more than three hundred miles after Jezebel threatened him. In those days, three hundred miles might as well have been three thousand miles. So with that much territory between him and jealous Jezebel, the panicky prophet finally stopped running.

The Danger of Feeling Indispensable

However, Elijah never let down his guard. Like a field mouse hiding from a hawk, "He went into a cave and spent the night. And the word of the Lord came to him: 'What are you doing here, Elijah?' He replied, 'I have been very zealous for the Lord God Almighty. The Israelites have rejected your covenant, broken down your altars, and put your prophets to death with the sword. I am the only one left, and now they are trying to kill me too'" (19:9–10).

Does this version of the situation strike you as a little arrogant? "I'm the only one left, God. If they take me, what will happen to your cause?" I wonder how many great works, founded under the direction of God, have folded because of one so-called indispensable man?

I know of one organization, greatly used of God, that was started by a man of faith and vision. He built it and developed it, but he couldn't let go of it. Thus, not only was he its founder and manager, he became its undertaker, too, for he ended up burying it. It is essential for every believer to understand that no one is indispensable to God. We are merely instruments in the hands of God. The Lord wants to use us. But the danger is that when He does use us, we sometimes begin to think that we are the ones causing the victory. Perhaps that is why God periodically removes an individual, in order to remind us afresh that this is not our work—it is His work.

A young man I'll call John was dead drunk on one of the destroyers anchored at Pearl Harbor on the morning of the Japanese attack. In the providence of God, his ship was not hit, and he survived the ordeal. Subsequent to that experience, John came to know Jesus Christ as his Savior through the serviceman's center in Honolulu. After the war, he finished college, came to the seminary, graduated, and became a naval chaplain.

During a ministry trip that I took to the islands, it was my privilege to get to know John more closely. He held three Sunday services in the chapel. At each one, more than three hundred men heard the gospel. Afterward, he invited a large group of servicemen to come home with us for dinner. After the meal, we sat around the living room, and for three or four hours John and I talked with the men about their questions.

That night, the chapel was packed to the doors for the evening service that John was leading. This, despite the competition of first-run movies for a dime on the base. But the men who showed up wanted to the Word of God. Some of them were driving clear across the island in order to get under the biblical teaching of this man.

I was scarcely back home in Dallas when I received a telegram from John's wife, Carol. This brilliant young man had been killed in a plane accident. He had gone to Guam to dedicate a new servicemen's center that he had been instrumental in starting. As the plane was taking off after the dedication service, it dropped into the jungle. Three days later the rescuers finally found the wreckage.

When I got that message, it was like being hit with a two-by-four. John left a wife and four children, all under the age of seven. Saddened beyond belief, I felt I had to write and offer some condolence to this grieving woman. That was one of the most difficult letters I have ever had to write. Among other things, I reminded Carol of God's promise: "all things work together for good" (Romans 8:28). I said, "God has underlined that little word 'together' in my mind. Things don't work in isolation, but 'together for good.'"

I don't know why God took John home. But I have to trust that He did the right thing, since the Lord has never proven to make mistakes in the past. As I reflected on his death, I thought of all the chaplains I had met over the years, some of whom had no concern for spiritual things or the Word of God. Yet here was a man with zeal—taken away! I think it was then that God began to teach me that the measure of a life is not its duration, but its contribution.

Suppose Jezebel had snuffed out the life of Elijah. Is it possible that his martyrdom might have galvanized the seven thousand prophets of the Lord who were hiding out in a cave (1 Kings 19:18)? We can only guess, but one thing is certain: no one is indispensable in God's service.

Elijah forgot that. He thought that somehow God's work could not be completed without him. So the Lord sent Elijah outside the cave. "Then a great and powerful wind tore the mountains apart and shattered the rocks before the Lord, but the Lord was not in the wind. After the wind there was an earthquake, but the Lord was not in the earthquake. After the earthquake was a fire, but the Lord was not in the fire. And after the fire came a gentle whisper. When Elijah heard it, he pulled his cloak over his face and went out and stood at the mouth of the cave" (19:11–13).

God finally got through to Elijah with a still, small voice. He wanted to teach the prophet that He not only speaks in the spectacular, He also speaks in silence. He not only communicates in glory, He also communicates in the grime.

Have you grasped that truth? Sometimes we get all caught up in a frenzy over the more highly publicized events in the cause of Christ—you know, the dynamic dramas that seemingly change the course of history. But what about the people God uses in the everyday regimen of life? It is easy to start thinking that God is only interested in that which is great. But God is interested in both great works and small. He calls us to follow Him whether He leads us in grand parade or an unknown journey. Earth-shattering events occur once in a while. But eternally significant events are swirling around us all the time in the warp and woof of everyday life.

Dr. Harry Ironside realized this. This eminent Bible teacher, always refreshing, used to visit the seminary quite often when I was a student there. I appreciated his down-to-earth approach to living the Christian life. One day I asked him, "Dr. Ironside, what do you think of all the teaching on the spiritual life?" I'll never forget his response: "It's fine if you've got a lot of time and money." You see, he didn't think much of complicated teaching when it came to Jesus Christ. He just wanted a real relationship that changed his life.

It took me a long time to appreciate his answer to my question. He was saying that the kind of spirituality that works is the kind in evidence on those nights when your kids come down with the stomach flu, or the car breaks down, or the plumbing backs up. If the Christian life works anywhere, it's got to work there. At least, that's the kind of Christianity I need, because that's the kind of life I lead.

To be on Mount Carmel is tremendously exciting. But most of us live on the plains and in the valleys. We live in the workplace, where godly values are often not honored. We live in schools and universities, where biblical truths are often not heard, even less taken seriously. We live in families, where Christlike love is often not practiced, causing pain and fractured relationships.

It is in these arenas that the still, small voice of God must become our confidence. It is here that we are called to live a life committed to Christ. Don't let the wiles of the enemy cut short your effectiveness.

CHAPTER SIX

Confidence

Every once in a while, you come across someone whose very confidence is inspiring. As a long-time fan of the Dallas Cowboys, I suffered for years as my team was routinely beaten by the San Francisco 49ers. However, even in the midst of defeat, I always enjoyed watching the cool, calm, collectedness of the 49ers' great quarterback, Joe Montana. The man just oozed confidence.

Whenever his team was in a tight spot—such as trailing in the fourth quarter with time running out—here would come Joe Montana, ready to engineer a comeback. After the victories, his teammates were always saying things like, "We knew we could win with Joe on the field. You could see it in his eyes. He just wouldn't allow us to lose." And it was true. He led his team to more last-minute, come-from-behind victories than any other player in the history of the game. He played with a certainty that he could win. And he had faith in his team, his coaches, and the game plan. As a result, he inspired confidence in every 49ers player and fan.

When we turn from sports to the arena of real life, we find that confidence is a quality that characterizes truly great people of God. Peter had it. Paul did, too. They and other biblical figures like them held onto a firm conviction that what they were doing was important—and, because God was leading them, it was the right thing to do.

Unfortunately, our culture has degraded confidence to the point where it is often confused with arrogance. But real confidence isn't simply self-confidence. It is a sense of certainty about the outcome. As the old quip puts it, it ain't braggin' if you can do it.

Of course, as Christians, we realize that we can't "do it." We can't live the Christian life all by ourselves, because as I've pointed out, the Christian life is not difficult, it's impossible, because it's supernatural. It is not us trying to produce a godly life, but God living His life through us. Therefore, we can say, confidence for the believer is not having faith in ourselves, but in someone greater than ourselves.

That is what makes the Christian unique. He isn't in the battle alone; the great Creator God is with him. He doesn't face the difficult situation by himself; the Holy Spirit is there to guide and empower him. When we realize that the Lord really is with us, and that His resources really are there to help us, we gain divine confidence that sees us through the most trying circumstances.

Elijah was a man of confidence. Not that he looked too confident in the previous chapter. Perhaps you thought he had retired, since after running away from Jezebel he more or less disappears from the Biblical record. But he wasn't retired—just resting up for his next assignment from God. Sure, he may have stumbled in his flight from the queen's fury, but his previous actions have already confirmed that Elijah was fundamentally confident in the Lord's power and purpose. That assurance, which he displays throughout his ministry, reveals five basic principles that ought to inspire and instruct us as we take part in our contest of life.

Renew Your Strength

The last time we saw Elijah, he was sitting outside a cave, straining to hear God's gentle whisper (1 Kings 19:12–13). After that, we don't hear about him again until 1 Kings 21:17 says, "Then the word of the Lord came to Elijah. . . ." The wording means, "after some time had passed." We don't know how much time that was. But we can easily surmise what Elijah was doing in that interval. He was resting, reflecting, and renewing his strength.

His need for that is obvious. When the angel met him under the broom tree, he was totally out of gas. The angel encouraged him to sleep, and gave him some food that kept him going another forty days and nights (19:5–8). But Elijah needed more than an all-expenses-paid vacation to Mount Horeb. He required a complete overhaul of his spirit, because his inner resources were depleted. Instead of ministering, he needed to be ministered to for a while.

This has been true for many of God's choice servants. For example, Moses, after rashly murdering an Egyptian and then running away to Midian, spent forty years learning the patience and quietness of a shepherd's life. Paul, after meeting Jesus Christ on the road to Damascus, spent a number of years in Arabia in order for God to prepare him for a life of useful service. Time out of the spotlight is often just what we need for the Lord to do His work in our lives. And nothing can take the place of that solitude. Some things just take time—and quiet. As we say in Texas, it takes nine months to have a baby; you can't put nine women on the job and get it done in a month.

Spending time on the bench may sound unproductive when there's still a game being played. But I believe almost every Christian needs that experience occasionally. If you are worried about whether the team can score points without you, I suggest that you reread the last chapter. Remember, no one is indispensable to God. He can get the job done through someone else. In fact, sometimes He insists on doing it that way, for their good *and yours*.

You see, while you are in "spiritual rehab," the Lord can help you refocus on Him. He can teach you truths to which you would never have paid attention otherwise. He can refresh your mind and spirit with a revitalized prayer life. And He can renew your strength by restoring your sense of purpose and mission.

But you don't necessarily need to wait for God to take you out of circulation. You can be wise about when is a good time for you to temporarily retreat. For example, whenever you have made an unusually difficult decision, gone through a period of extreme stress, or emerged from a major crisis, you would probably do well to "drop out" for a while. You don't have to completely let go of every responsibility and commitment. That may not be practical or wise. But you can decline taking on any new commitments, and you can scale back and simplify life so as to allow the whisper of God to speak into your life.

Of course, the one group that ought to honor this principle more than any other—pastors, missionaries, and other vocational Christian workers—tends to be the group that most violates it. That's tragic, because there is nothing quite as draining as public ministry. I can assure you, ministry can be hard work. If you are a layperson, you may look at your pastor and think, "He doesn't have it so bad. A couple hours of work on Sunday morning. Maybe an evening service, too. A Wednesday night talk. A funeral here. A wedding there. What's so tough about that?" But that sort of thinking indicates a lack of awareness.

H.B. London, assistant to the president at Focus on the Family, cites a Fuller Institute of Church Growth Study that found that 90 percent of pastors work more than 46 hours a week; 90 percent feel that they are inadequately trained to cope with ministry demands; 50 percent feel unable to meet the needs of the job; 75 percent report a significant stress-related crisis at least once in their ministry; 80 percent believe that pastoral ministry has a negative affect on their families; and 33 percent say that being in the ministry is downright hazardous to their families (*Pastors at Risk*, p. 22). Clearly, the pastorate is no bed of roses.

I can speak about that from personal experience, having been a pastor, a seminary professor, and a preacher and Bible teacher. The demands of ministry drain me physically, emotionally, and spiritually. Sometimes after classes on Friday I'll catch a plane and fly somewhere to do a conference or seminar. I may speak twice on Friday night, twice on Saturday morning, hold a workshop Saturday afternoon, and then speak once or twice Saturday evening. Then on Sunday, I might preach in the sponsoring church; if they have two or three services, that means preaching the sermon two or three times. Then they'll sometimes pull together a meeting in the afternoon, and then I'll go speak at the evening service. All told, I may give a dozen presentations in the course of a weekend—and that's hoping they don't hold me over until Monday! Needless to say, by the time I get back on the plane to go home, I am one exhausted preacher.

I remember one time I ran into a friend at church who heard I had been out on one of these ministry junkets. "Hey, Howie," he said, "Welcome back. How was your vacation?"

I'm sure it was the grace of God that restrained me from throttling him! But I figured out a way to set him straight. "Oh, it was fantastic," I told him. "In fact, why don't you go with me next time."

"Could I?" he replied, all excited. He thought that would be a fun thing to do. So a few weeks later I took him with me on a three-day trip. By the time we got back, I was carrying *his* bags, he was so worn out. "Boy, Howie, I'm going to have to take a week off to get over this," he told me.

I just smiled and nodded, but inside I was thinking, "How in the world can you be worn out? *I'm* the one who had to do the speaking!"

Over time, that kind of grueling pace takes its toll. A few years back, I worked myself into a situation where I was simply too busy. It seemed as if I was going every minute, stepping from one plane to another, getting up in front of one crowd or another. After awhile, I wasn't even sure what city I was in, or who I was speaking to. I grew physically fatigued, mentally flabby, and spiritually wasted. I felt as if I'd said everything I ever had to say. There was just nothing left.

That's when I was reminded of what Jesus did when He had a crushing schedule: "The people brought to Jesus all the sick and demon-possessed. The whole town gathered at the door, and Jesus healed many. . . very early in the morning, while it was still dark, Jesus got up, left the house and went off to a solitary place, where he prayed" (Mark 1:32–35).

So I followed the example of the Master. I carved a few days out of my schedule and went off to a quiet place in the country. I didn't take any ministry books, just my Bible. I took a few walks, spent time with Jeanne, and allowed the Lord to minister to me. Like Elijah, I was worn out and in need of renewal. And like Elijah, I found God restoring my strength.

Remember His Work

Elijah spent time out of commission. But eventually God called him back into service. The Lord said, "Go down to meet Ahab king of Israel, who rules in Samaria. He is now in Naboth's vineyard" (1 Kings 21:18).

Do you recall the last time Elijah had been in the presence of Ahab? It was just after the Lord's dramatic victory over Baal on Mount Carmel. Ahab mounted his chariot and rode off in a rage, and soon his wife brought threats against Elijah. No doubt these memories came to mind when the prophet was told to go to the king once again.

I know of only one thing that would give a person confidence to follow through with that assignment: remembering what God has done in the past. I say this because failing to remember God's works inevitably leads to a failure of faith.

Consider Israel as a case in point. The nation had every reason to constantly praise God for His incredible provision on their behalf. For instance, He miraculously opened up the Red Sea to allow the people to leave Egypt. He led them through the wilderness with a pillar of fire. He repeatedly routed their enemies. He graciously provided manna each morning, and even produced water from a rock on a couple of occasions. All these works and more the Lord performed for His people. Yet after each one, the Israelites quickly forgot about His blessing and moved on to the next complaint. As a result, their spiritual confidence dwindled, and when they were confronted with the crucial choice of going up and taking possession of the Promised Land, their faith faltered.

Now it's easy for us to criticize these Hebrews for their lack of trust in God. But are we much different? How many times do we find ourselves doubting God and His concern for us, even though He has provided for us countless times in the past? Do we remember His goodness to us? Do we celebrate the history of His grace?

I have seen churches struggle for years to pay off a mortgage, then when they finally do, they hold one little service and then they move on to some new project. Likewise, many church leaders are goal-oriented people who just can't seem to stop and enjoy success. As soon as they accomplish one goal, they drop their interest in it in order to move on to the next one. Is that honoring to God? No, we need to pause and celebrate what He has done, and really enjoy His blessings. Otherwise, we are liable to forget His works.

It was for this reason that later generations of Israelites composed the psalms. They didn't want to forget God's great works, so they set them to music. That way, they could teach their children to sing of the wonderful things that the Lord had done. For example (Psalm 66:5–6),

> Come and see what God has done,
>> how awesome His works in man's behalf!
> He turned the sea into dry land,
>> they passed through the river on foot—
>> come, let us rejoice with Him.

Psalms 78, 106, 136, and many others illustrate the principle that confidence in God is gained by recalling His works. Refresh your memory about what God has done in the past, and you will rekindle your faith for what He will do in the future.

When our children were small, we made sure they heard stories about God's faithfulness to His people. For instance, in our family devotions we read *Through Gates of Splendor*, the story of the five missionaries who gave their lives to take the gospel to the Auca Indians. On another occasion we read *Pilgrim's Progress*. And of course Jeanne and I told of our own personal relationship with the Lord, and the many times when He superintended in our lives. We wanted to build a confidence in our children that God could be trusted, and that He is present in the lives of His people.

We were not just telling stories. We were building a foundation of faith. We were following the biblical model laid down by Asaph (Psalm 78:2–7):

I will open my mouth in parables,
    I will utter hidden things, things from of old—
what we have heard and known,
    what our fathers have told us.
We will not hide them from their children;
    we will tell the next generation
the praiseworthy deeds of the LORD,
    his power, and the wonders he has done.
He decreed statutes for Jacob
    and established the law in Israel,
which he commanded our forefathers
    to teach their children,
so the next generation would know them,
    even the children yet to be born,
    and they in turn would tell their children.
Then they would put their trust in God

and would not forget his deeds
but would keep his commands.

Remain in Him

Imagine for a moment that you are standing in Elijah's shoes. God has spoken to you, saying, "Go down to meet King Ahab. . .Say to him, 'This is what the Lord says: Have you not murdered a man and seized his property?' Then say to him, 'This is what the Lord says: In the place where dogs licked up Naboth's blood, dogs will lick up your blood— yes, yours!'" (1 Kings 21:19). That's a pretty strong message to present to a king. It's bound to be greeted with a hostile reception. Where can you find the strength to deliver it?

None of us likes to be the bearer of bad news. Having to fire an employee, fail a student, inform a customer that his check has bounced, tell a patient he's got a terminal illness—situations like these can be extremely hard. So we often try to couch our woeful message in positive terms. For example, I recently read a management book that told employers never to "fire" anyone but to "release them into a more positive job environment." I wonder if that sort of approach would have worked for Elijah. Perhaps he could have put a positive spin on the Lord's dire words: "I've got good news, King Ahab. Your dogs are going to be very well fed!"

No, the only way one can have the strength of character to deliver a message of judgment is to hold fast to the knowledge that what you are saying is from God. Elijah did not have to worry about acting as a messenger as long as he remembered whose message he was bringing.

A similar circumstance occurred in Daniel's day. A group of evil officials schemed to convince King Darius to pass a law against praying to the Lord. Daniel immediately recognized this decision as being directly opposed to his faith. The Bible tells us, "Now when Daniel learned that the decree had been published, he went home to his upstairs room where the windows opened toward Jerusalem. Three times a day he got down on his knees and prayed, giving thanks to God" (Daniel 6:10).

You can't help but admire Daniel for his courage. Fully aware that these men were trying to entrap him, he not only continued praying to the Lord, he prayed with his windows open so everyone could see and hear him! He knew what the punishment would be—being thrown into a den of lions. But he prayed anyway. Frankly, I doubt that he knew he was going to be spared by God. He knew that God had the power to protect him, but there is nothing in the text to suggest that he expected a miraculous deliverance. Thus he willingly risked death in order to obey the Lord. How did he come by that boldness? He spent so much time in the Lord's presence that he remained confident in Him, whether it meant life or death.

I have known Christians like that, people who faced financial ruin, physical danger, and psychological persecution for holding fast to godliness. The only way they have held up under that kind of opposition is by remaining close to Jesus Christ.

Remember Jesus' words to His followers, just before he went to the cross? In the upper room he told them, "Remain in me, and I will remain in you. No branch can bear fruit by itself; it must remain in the vine. Neither can you bear fruit unless you remain in me" (John 15:4). That's the key to being an effective representative of the Lord—remaining in Him.

Respect Others

As we examine the life of Elijah, it is easy to overlook his respectful attitude. Here is a man who came against kings and called down fire from heaven. We think of him as bold, daring, and full of dramatic eloquence.

Certainly on Mount Carmel he had a flair for the dramatic. But in delivering the Lord's message to King Ahab, we find him respectful, not rude, restrained, not rowdy. Not that anyone could blame Elijah if he blasted the king, since Ahab greeted him with icy irritation: "So you have found me, my enemy!" (1 Kings 21:20). Furthermore, the king was no one to respect, for as the author of 1 Kings informs us, "there was never a man like Ahab, who sold himself to do evil in the eyes of the Lord, urged on by Jezebel his wife. He behaved in the vilest manner. . . ." (21:25–26).

Nevertheless, Elijah spoke softly, though sternly, to Ahab: "I have found you." (21:20). Without further provoking the situation, he quietly delivered God's message to the king, showing him consideration that few thought he deserved.

In response, Ahab did something totally unexpected—he humbled himself before the Lord (21:27). Who knows what Elijah must have been thinking as he observed Ahab's repentance? It would have been understandable if Elijah had rejected the king's behavior as insincere. But there is no suggestion that he did. Perhaps he realized that he was not the one to judge Ahab's heart. Perhaps, too, he remembered that even wicked kings can find forgiveness from a gracious God if they humble themselves and turn from their evil ways.

Treating others with respect is a mark of confidence. Show me a bully who has to push people around, and I'll show you a very insecure individual. By contrast, the person who treats others with deference displays a self-mastery that indicates confidence. He is in control of himself, so he doesn't need to brow-beat others to gain control.

The supreme example of this respectful attitude is the Lord Jesus. He had authority to make even the winds and the rains obey him. Yet He humbled Himself before the authorities of His day. "When they hurled insults at Him, He did not retaliate. When He suffered, He made no threats" (1 Peter 2:23).

Likewise, when Peter and John were seized by the temple guard and hauled before the Sanhedrin for preaching Christ, they were warned "not to speak or teach at all in the name of Jesus" (Acts 4:18). I love their respectful attitude. They didn't whine. They didn't complain. They didn't try to manipulate the court. Instead they politely but boldly replied, "Judge for yourselves whether it is right in God's sight to obey you rather than God. For we cannot help speaking about what we have seen and heard" (Acts 4:19–20).

"Manner and message are inextricably linked," observes David Roper. "One goes with the other. Without kindness, truth is just so much dogma. Without truth, kindness is mere sentimentality. Only God's truth delievered with loving kindness has power to bring about consent."

Respect doesn't come from being the toughest guy on the block. Ahab was one of the toughest characters in the Old Testament, but few had much regard for him. People may have feared him; no one respected him. No, it was Elijah who gained universal acclaim and standing. Why? Because he held his ground for the Lord. As a result, he was able to treat even his nemesis Ahab with a respect he did not deserve. He illustrated the truth of Isaiah, that "the effect of righteousness will be quietness and confidence forever" (Isaiah 32:17).

Re-Present God

Earlier we saw that much of Elijah's boldness came from the conviction that he was a representative of the Lord. In other words, he stood for God when he stood before Ahab. He "re-presented" God to the king.

Obviously, God could have revealed Himself to Ahab in some sort of direct encounter, as He did with Nebuchadnezzar, king of Babylon, or with Saul on the road to Damascus. But I wonder whether Ahab could have survived the experience. His character had slipped so far, his spirituality was so degenerate, that I think he would have keeled over if ever he found himself in the presence of the Almighty. So it was gracious of God to use an intermediary.

It was also effective. Whereas earlier confrontations between the prophet and this profligate king had proven unfruitful, the message of judgment somehow hit home this time: "When Ahab heard these words, he tore his clothes, put on sackcloth and fasted. He lay in sackcloth and went around meekly" (1 Kings 21:27). Clearly, Ahab got the picture. He finally realized that he was dealing with the living God. Elijah had re-presented God effectively.

Have you ever considered that God is calling you to re-present Him in your sphere of influence? Paul informs us that "the god of this age has blinded the minds of unbelievers, so that they cannot see the light of the gospel of the glory of Christ" (2 Corinthians 4:4). Are you aware of that? All around you are people who are stumbling around in spiritual darkness because they've never seen God. How are they going to see him? Paul tells us: "For God, who said, 'Let light shine out of darkness,' made his light shine *in our hearts*" (4:6, emphasis added). In other words, unbelievers see God to the extent that they see him in you and me.

That doesn't sound too hopeful, does it? Because if you are like me, you tend to think, "Don't look at me! I'm no paragon of spirituality. I don't look very much like Christ. I've got too many faults, too many flaws, too many failures to have anyone look at me and find God."

Fortunately, the Holy Spirit anticipated that anxiety, because He inspired the apostle to add a disclaimer: "But we have this treasure in jars of clay to show that this all-surpassing power is from God and not from us" (4:7). That's a comforting thought! What gives spiritual sight to the unbeliever is the light of Christ, not the vessel that contains the light.

I remember visiting a woman's home one time and sitting in her beautifully appointed living room. I think she must have been an interior decorator, because every piece of furniture, every piece of art on the walls, every drape, every cushion, every fiber of carpet was exquisitely arranged. Yet as I glanced around this tastefully arranged room, my eyes fell on a bouquet of flowers sitting on the coffee table in front of me. It was not the flowers that attracted my attention, but the container in which they were placed—a beat up old mayonnaise jar! I could hardly believe it. What in the world was this piece of junk doing in here, I thought.

Just then my hostess entered the room with her five-year-old daughter. "Howie, I want you to meet Christine. She was so excited to hear that you were coming all the way from Texas. She thinks Texas is full of cactus and sand (it isn't!), so she picked these flowers to show you what they look like. I'm afraid she just grabbed the first thing she could find to put them in. But no matter. The flowers are lovely!"

They were lovely indeed. Later I thought, that's what Paul meant when he talked about God's treasures being in earthen vessels. It's the treasures that matter, not the vessels. We are nothing but mayonnaise jars in which the beauty of Christ needs to be displayed. Is that your commit-ment—to be God's mayonnaise jar, a humble but available vessel through which He can re-present Himself to a world that desperately needs to know what He looks like?

PART TWO

Serving Your Generation

CHAPTER SEVEN

Mentoring

I n 1919, a young man recovering from injuries suffered in the Great War in Europe rented a small apartment in Chicago. He chose the location for its proximity to the home of Sherwood Anderson, the famous author. Anderson had penned the widely praised novel *Winesburg, Ohio*, and was known for his willingness to help younger writers.

The two men became fast friends and spent nearly every day together for two years. They shared meals, took long walks, and discussed the craft of writing late into the night. The younger man often brought samples of his work to Anderson, and the veteran author responded by giving brutally honest critiques. Yet the young writer was never deterred. Each time, he would listen, take careful notes, and then return to his typewriter to improve his material. He didn't try to defend himself, for, as he put it later, "I didn't know how to write until I met Sherwood Anderson."

One of the most helpful things Anderson did for his young protégé was to introduce him to his network of associates in the publishing world. Soon, the younger man was writing on his own. In 1926, he published his first novel, which met with critical acclaim. Its title was *The Sun Also Rises*, and the author's name was Ernest Hemingway.

But wait! The story doesn't end there. After Hemingway left Chicago, Anderson moved to New Orleans. There he met another young wordsmith, a poet with an insatiable drive to improve his skills. Anderson put him through the same paces he had put Hemingway—writing, critiquing, discussing, encouraging—and always more writing. He gave the young man copies of his novels and encouraged him to read them carefully, noting the words, themes, and development of character and story. A year later, Anderson helped this man publish his first novel, *Soldier Pay*. Three years later, this bright new talent, William Faulkner, produced *The Sound and the Fury*, and it quickly became an American masterpiece.

Anderson's role as a mentor to aspiring authors didn't stop there. In California, he spent several years working with playwright Thomas Wolfe and a young man named John Steinbeck, among others. All told, three of Anderson's protégés earned Nobel Prizes and four Pulitzer Prizes for literature. The famous literary critic Malcolm Cowley said that Anderson was "the only writer of his generation to leave his mark on the style and vision of the next generation."

What caused Anderson to so generously give of his time and expertise to help younger people? One reason might be that he himself had sat under the influence of an older writer, the great Theodore Dreiser. He also spent considerable time with Carl Sandburg.

I find this pattern instructive. Not only does it mirror my own experience, it also illustrates what I have found to be a fundamental principle of human experience—that the greatest means of impacting the future is to build into another person's life. This process is called *mentoring*.

"Mentoring" is not a word you will find in Scripture, but the principle is found throughout. In fact, we need look no further than the relationship between the prophet Elijah and his successor, Elisha, to see a prime illustration.

Let's go back to that cave where Elijah heard God in a whisper. Do you remember his state of mind? He was drained, distressed, and despondent: "I am the only one left," he told the Lord, "and now they are trying to kill me too" (1 Kings 19:14).

He was only half right. His life was in danger, true. But the Lord revealed that no less than seven thousand people had not given in to the worship of Baal. One of these, the Lord mentioned by name: "Anoint Elisha son of Shaphat from Abel Meholah to succeed you as prophet" (19:16).

The tendency of many upon reading this instruction is to assume that Elijah was finished. It's as if God were saying, "Look, Elijah, I don't need you anymore. I've got a new man to get the job done. In fact, on your way out, why don't you go tell him that he'll be serving as your replacement?"

However, let me offer a different interpretation—one with a great deal more hope. By naming Elijah's successor, God was showing Himself faithful. He was telling Elijah that his efforts had not been in vain. There would be a future. In fact, Elijah would have the privilege of ushering in that future by passing the torch to Elisha.

To my mind, this is the chief benefit of mentoring another individual: by doing so, we leave a legacy for those who follow after us. As long as the Lord tarries, every one of us is going to check out sooner or later. There's a 100 percent certainty of that. So the question becomes, what will we leave behind? Most people answer that question by establishing a will. But my friend, a will only disposes of the junk you've accumulated over the years. The deeper question is, what is there of *you* that will pass on to the next generation?

Not long ago, a man named Walt passed away in the city of

Philadelphia. Walt had a family, but none of particular celebrity. He had few possessions, for he had never saved much as a tool and dye worker, a trade from which he was long retired. He left no books or other significant writings, for he had never made it past the sixth grade. In short, Walt's death barely made a ripple in the tide of human history. I doubt the obituaries gave him more than a few cursory lines to note his passing.

But believe it or not, Walt had and continues to have a profound impact for the cause of Christ. That's really all he ever wanted. You see, in his younger days, Walt started a Sunday school class for boys. It was not an especially large class, nor was the church in which it was held an especially noteworthy congregation. Yet out of 13 boys in Walt's class, 11 entered vocational Christian work, of whom several remain active today. I know, because I'm one of them.

I call that a legacy! But it didn't just happen. Walt created that legacy by building into the lives of young men who needed a teacher, a guide, a coach, a father-figure, an older friend. That's what a mentor is—a person who helps another person develop and grow. It may be through a formal relationship, as in a professor working with a student, or it may be more informal, as in Walt's work with a group of boys. In either case, mentoring involves a relationship in which one person invests himself in the life of another.

That's what God was asking Elijah to do, because Israel would still need a prophet after Elijah departed the scene. In our own day, I believe God is asking you and me to serve as mentors, because there will still be a need for godly people when we depart the scene.

The need has never been greater. For example, consider that tonight 40 percent of the children in America will go to bed in homes where their biological father is not present. So writes David Blankenhorn in his chilling study, *Fatherless America*. Whereas only 6 percent of homes in 1950 were female-headed with no male present, today that figure has exploded to 24 percent. Indeed, in many inner-city neighborhoods, *live-at-home fathers are extinct!*

Who is going to model fatherhood for the children of these homes? Who is going to show them what it means for a man to be committed to them? Who is going to teach the boys especially—who are in the same, exact predicament I was, growing up—what it means to be a man? Thank God I had Walt! Apart from him, I could have lived, died, and gone to a Christless eternity, and no one might have cared. But I am who I am today thanks in large measure to the influence of that man.

But it's not just the children of broken homes who need mentors. The children of solid homes need them as well. Jeanne and I might like to think we gave our four children everything they needed in life. But realistically, we know that we didn't. We couldn't. No parent can. Even the best parents need other adults to supply for their children what they are unable to pass along—skills that they do not have, habits that they have not cultivated, wisdom that they do not possess, experience that they cannot offer. Those are the kinds of things a mentor can supply.

And when we turn to the church, we find an unparalleled need for mentoring. As a seminary professor, I'm privileged to observe the leading edge of future Christian leaders as they come up through the ranks. But several years ago, I made a troubling discovery: few of these bright young people have ever had mentors. I hear the same story from student after student: "Prof, I've never had someone to look up to. I've never had someone build into my life."

I hear the same thing from men in the Promise Keepers movement, of which I'm delighted to be a part. As I've spoken on the subject of mentoring at a number of the gatherings and leadership training events, man after man has told me, "I'd give *anything* for a mentor! Where can I find one?"

I'm encouraged by the desire for mentoring, but I find such a widespread and long-term lack of it distressing, because mentoring relationships are a primary means by which believers grow into maturity. You see, many of us in the church are under the mistaken impression that the way to produce spiritually mature Christians is to enroll people in a course on spiritual maturity. We give them books on the subject. We take them to passages of Scripture. We hand out assignments and worksheets. Nothing wrong with these activities. But has it ever occurred to you that spiritual growth is rarely the product of assimilating more information?

If it were, we could have transformed the world several million books ago. But inasmuch as knowing Christ involves a *relationship*, growing in Christ also involves relationships. One of the most helpful of these involves a mentor. That's because most of us don't need to know more nearly as much as we need to *be known* more. We don't need a set of principles to practice nearly as much as we need another *person* to help us. We need someone to believe in us, stand by us, guide us, model Christ for us. We need another's encouragement, wisdom, example, and accountability. We need his smiles, his hugs, his frowns, his tears.

I believe this is what Elijah gave to Elisha. Scripture does not give us all the details of their relationship. But let me suggest three ways in which Elijah mentored his successor—and in the process set a wonderful pattern for those of us today who need to be influencing a younger generation.

First, *Elijah took the initiative.* Verse 19 is clear: "So Elijah went from there and found Elisha." I like that! In obedience to the Lord's instruction, the prophet actively sought out Elisha, found him plowing in his field, and threw his cloak around him as a symbol that Elisha would succeed him as prophet. Elijah was *proactive.* He didn't just wait for Elisha to come to him, with the attitude, "I'm the master. If this fellow wants to follow in my footsteps, let him show how smart he is by coming to me and asking for my help." No, he went searching for his successor. And when he found him, he made his intentions clear.

We could use a lot more of that today. As I say, wherever I go, I hear younger people asking, "Where can I find a mentor?" At the same time, I hear older people asking, "Where can I find a ministry?" Could there be a more obvious connection? But the truth of the matter is, not many mentoring relationships will be established unless the older people take initiative to seek out the younger and make themselves available. Why? Because many potential protégés are intimidated by the process. They are afraid to ask for help. Some are afraid of rejection. Others aren't even aware of their potential. So for an older person to come along and befriend that younger person is a tremendous step forward.

By the way, let me let you in on a little secret: many people who are qualified to serve as mentors are intimidated by the mentoring process, too. Many are standing on the sidelines, thinking, "I don't have anything to offer. I've never been trained. What will I say?" But if you have any substantive experience in the faith, and if you have learned any lessons in life, you actually have far more to offer than you realize. Remember, mentoring is not so much a matter of transfering information as it is coming alongside another person to serve them in their development.

"But who should I approach?" you may be wondering. The Lord made it plain who Elijah's successor was going to be. How can the rest of us identify someone to mentor? In a moment we'll look at some qualities in Elisha that will help to answer that question. But I suggest that the first thing you do is pray. Remember that Elijah was known for his prayer life. Therefore, it is altogether likely that he had spent considerable time in prayer asking God to indicate who should take up his mantel as the next prophet to Israel. If so, the Lord's instruction outside the cave on Mount Horeb was God's response to Elijah's prayer.

Once you have asked God to show you a prospective protégé, open your eyes and look for someone who gives evidence that he wants to grow. It may be something he says. It may be his eagerness or teachability. But see if there's a *desire* to develop.

I well recall a student a number of years ago who invariably sat on the front row in every single class he ever took from me. He regularly had his hand up, firing away with questions—some of the most perceptive I've ever been asked. After class he would be up front plying me with more questions. Then I'd run into him on campus and he'd grab me for another round of give and take. Meanwhile, his papers and assignments showed not only keen interest in the material, but practical application of it to his walk with Christ. Needless to say, I had no trouble wanting to make time for this individual. He obviously was motivated in terms of his training and development. His name? Charles Swindoll. Today, Chuck is president of the seminary where I teach and known internationally for his insight into God's Word.

I could tell of many others like Chuck whom I've been privileged to influence over the years. One element they shared in common was the desire to grow. Whenever I saw that, it was hard for me not to make myself available. That's why I suggest that you look for that quality in the men and women God brings into your sphere of influence—at your church, in your neighborhood, in your community, where you work. Whenever you see someone eager to grow spiritually and personally, ask yourself, what can I do to help? It may be that this individual is someone the Lord wants you to mentor.

This brings us to the second thing that Elijah did to mentor Elisha: *he made himself available.* After Elijah ceremoniously tapped Elisha by wrapping him in his cloak, the text says the young farmer "left his oxen and ran after Elijah" (19:20). Later, after saying goodbye to his parents, Elisha "set out to follow Elijah and became his attendant" (19:21). In this manner, Elisha attached himself to Elijah, and it becomes evident that the seasoned prophet spent considerable time grooming his young protégé.

Most of his influence was the result of the relationship. How do I know that? Because there were no books or audio or videotape series in that day. "All" that Elijah had to offer was himself. Frankly, that was a blessing. It forced the two men to deal with each other eyeball to eyeball. Nowadays, unless someone's got a best-selling book out or a radio program or a seminar, he almost assumes he can't have an impact. But I've discovered that while these are excellent means of conveying concepts, nothing can take the place of a heart-to-heart relationship. So if you are not an eloquent communicator, take heart! You can still have an incredible influence simply by sharing of yourself.

But that's going to require time. And of course, as soon as I say that, I can hear prospective mentors bailing out right and left. "I'm too busy already!" they'll say. But wait! When I talk about mentoring, I'm not asking you to add to an already crowded schedule. Believe me, I understand that predicament firsthand! But instead of trying to cram one more demand into your life, I am suggesting that you act more strategically in the relationships you already have.

For example, let's say that there's a young fellow who just hired on where you work, and in the course of conversation, you've discovered that he is passionately in love with the Savior. He really wants to go for broke in terms of his spiritual experience. Could you be of assistance? Quite possibly—and not necessarily with a demand on your time. After all, you are going to eat lunch every day anyway, right? Why not invite this young man to share that mealtime with you? You don't have to have a high-powered agenda (unless you both agree to that). You can simply talk about the things you have in common—your faith in Christ and what it means to walk with Him. I guarantee, over time you can make a profound difference in that individual's life, not just by what you say, but by the fact that you care and pay attention. Remember, mentoring is a relationship, not an item to check off a to-do list.

There's a third thing that Elijah did to influence young Elisha: *he served as a model.* To me, this is the most powerful part of the mentoring process. You see, as the eminent researcher Albert Bandura showed, modeling is the most far-reaching form of unconscious learning there is. People will forget most of what you say; they will forget almost nothing of what you do. Therefore, whatever behavior you model for your protégé is the pattern he will tend to follow—or, in some cases, reject.

Elijah gave Elisha plenty of opportunity to observe him in action. We don't know exactly how much time transpired between the call of Elisha and the dramatic departure of Elijah in the fiery chariot (2 Kings

2:1–12), but we do know that throughout that period, Elisha was regularly in Elijah's company. That means he must have been there when Elijah confronted Ahab concerning the murder of Naboth, and watched as Ahab repented and humbled himself before the Lord (1 Kings 21:17–29). Likewise, he must have tagged along when Elijah was sent to Ahab's son Ahaziah to chastise him for consulting Philistine idols instead of the Lord God of Israel (2 Kings 1:1–17). Those were but two of the countless experiences the two men shared together. Can you imagine how much Elisha must have gained by the exposure?

In a similar way, what could someone gain by hanging around you? Perhaps they could learn what it means to pray when faced with a problem or a crisis; or what faithfulness to a spouse is all about; or what a biblical work ethic looks like; or the process of introducing an unbeliever to the gospel; or the bittersweet task of saying goodbye to someone who is dying. There are countless opportunities every day for you to model Christlikeness to a younger believer. Are you allowing anyone the benefit of sharing these experiences with you?

However, let's jump to the other side of the relationship and consider mentoring from the perspective of the protégé. Perhaps you identify more with Elisha than Elijah in that you would like to be mentored before you try to mentor someone else. If so, notice several things that Elisha brought to the relationship.

First of all, he was *motivated*. We've already seen that when Elijah called him, "Elisha left his oxen and ran after Elijah" (19:20). In other words, he dropped what he was doing in order to follow after this man of God. Furthermore, he didn't just wander over to the prophet; he *ran* after him, as though he couldn't wait to spend time with him. This response indicates that Elisha was eager to accept the challenge of growth.

Are you? I had a guy come to me once to talk about his marriage. We spent quite some time discussing the problems of the relationship. Then we decided on three or four practical things he could do right away to improve the situation. The next week, he was back in my office with the same complaints.

"Did you try any of the things I suggested?" I asked him.

"What things?" he replied.

So we waded through it all over again. Finally, after he agreed on what he could do, I sent him on his way. But when he returned the next week—you guessed it—he was back to the same old story! Still struggling, still hadn't acted on any of our agreements.

"I don't think I can help you," I told him. In fact, no one could help a person like that. He wanted to whine, but he didn't want to work. He wanted to talk theoretically about his problems, but he didn't want to take practical action to solve them.

How different was the response of Elisha! Here was a young man who was eager to take responsibility for his growth.

A second quality that marked Elisha as a promising protégé was his *humility*. The text says that Elisha became Elijah's "attendant" (19:21). Elsewhere in the Old Testament, that word is translated as "servant" or "minister," as when the boy Samuel is said to have "ministered before the Lord under Eli the priest" (1 Samuel 2:11). The idea is that Elisha served Elijah. He sought to meet his needs, even as he learned from him.

That attitude of a servant requires humility. We can well imagine that if Elisha had been a lesser man, he easily could have gotten puffed up once he realized that the mantle of leadership would eventually fall on him: "Hey, I'm going to be the Lord's point man pretty soon. I'm going to be the one to call down fire from heaven. I'm set! I don't need to hang around this old guy. He's past his prime anyway." Instead, Elisha took the part of a servant, attending to the needs of his mentor.

Friend, I don't know how much talent you may have, but I do know that talent without humility is like a drunk at the wheel of a car. It's an accident waiting to happen. The way to prevent a crash like that is to bring yourself under the discipline of a seasoned, mature individual and take the part of a servant. That doesn't mean ignoring the gifts God has given you. It means filtering them through an attitude of meekness. Once you have proven yourself trustworthy in the small things, you will be ready to step up to more advanced responsibilities.

Paul advised his own protégé Timothy, "The things you have heard me say in the presence of many witnesses entrust to *reliable* men" (2 Timothy 2:2, emphasis added). His point is, don't be too quick to hand out leadership and responsibility based on talent alone. Also consider whether the person is liable to let his newfound opportunities go to his head.

You can always spot a humble person. He's the one who doesn't know everything. Some people already have an answer for every problem. Thus they are totally unteachable. But the humble individual recognizes that he still has room to grow. He is willing to admit that he can still learn from someone else—especially someone who has been down the road a bit farther than he has. That's the sort of person who is ready for the help of a mentor.

There's a final quality that we need to notice about Elisha: he was incredibly *loyal*. He stayed with Elijah until the very end. Three times he was given an opportunity to leave, but each time he replied, "As surely as the Lord lives and as you live, I will not leave you" (2 Kings 2:2, 4, 6).

Loyalty reveals much about a person's character. Earlier I related that Ernest Hemingway learned to write by spending time with Sherwood Anderson. There's a sad punch line to that story. After achieving international fame, Hemingway poked fun at his mentor. He ridiculed him publicly, perhaps as a way to show that he was now out from under Anderson's shadow. But it was shameful behavior, and Hemingway never quite came to terms with what he had done. Years later, he finally gave credit to his predecessor, but he always seemed to shy away from apologizing. I find that tragic, because it is clear from Hemingway's writing that he understood the value of loyalty. Unfortunately, his behavior belied his understanding.

Loyalty in a protégé is crucial, because the mentoring relationship is a two-way street. Just as you place confidence in your mentor, so he is placing a measure of trust in you. He is giving of his time, his wisdom, his expertise, his network, his money, or his other resources. In doing so, he is saying, "I believe in you. I am counting on you to take these gifts and use them to become the man or woman God made you to be." That kind of investment saddles you with responsibility. You will show what sort of person you are by how you handle that trust.

Some have defined mentoring as the process whereby an older person helps a younger person succeed. There's a measure of truth in that, but I prefer to see mentoring in slightly different terms. Rather than being about success, mentoring is about significance. The difference is that success means reaching your goals, whereas significance involves making a difference in the lives of people. How many of us achieve our objectives, yet still are left wondering whether our lives really count for anything?

That's why I'm bullish on mentoring relationships. It proves significant for both the mentor and the person being mentored. The last time Elijah and Elisha were together, Elisha saw the prophet being taken away in a fiery chariot and a whirlwind (2 Kings 2:11). Who can say what Elijah was thinking at that moment? I suspect that all thoughts of the world were quickly falling away! Nevertheless, Elijah must have come to the end of his life with a profound sense of significance. It was not just that he had accomplished great things. He had, but more than that, he was leaving a legacy—the legacy of a man into whose life he had poured his own. Having experienced something of that myself, I can tell you that few things are more gratifying.

As for Elisha, he, too, took away a profound sense of significance from the relationship. We know that by his first words after picking up Elijah's mantle: "Where now is the Lord, the God of Elijah?" (2:14). That's beautiful! It indicates that Elisha inherited more than Elijah's job as prophet; he gained a sense of the Almighty. No one could ask for more than that.

Are you looking for a closer walk with Christ? If so, I suggest that you seek out a mentor. He can never replace the Savior, but he just might tell you where you can find Him in your own experience.

CHAPTER EIGHT

Ministry

O ne of the great misnomers of our day is the word "minister." People use it as a synonym for the ordained clergy, but they reveal a fundamental misunderstanding when they do. They might be surprised to learn that "minister" derives from the Latin word for "servant" or "attendant," and is based on the root word *minus*, which means "less." Technically, then, a "minister" is someone of "lesser" rank or status, someone whose job it is to serve, not to be served.

I'm not suggesting that modern-day clergy and other vocational Christian workers are not servants. But I do perceive that most people— even most Christians—think of the clergy as God's "first team," carrying out His significant work, while the laity sort of comprise the cheering section.

But this is a far cry from the biblical perspective. If you turn to

Ephesians 4, you will find four categories of gifted people singled out—apostles, prophets, evangelists, and pastor-teachers. Elsewhere in the New Testament, we learn that every believer has been gifted by the Holy Spirit (for example, 1 Corinthians 12:7). But here, Paul identifies these four gifts as having a particular function: "to prepare God's people for works of service" (Ephesians 4:12).

Two key truths emerge from this passage. First, it is God's people, commonly called the laity (*laos*, "people"), to whom the "works of service" have been given. In other words, ministry belongs primarily to laypeople, not to the clergy. In fact—and this is the second truth—the main task that God has given to the clergy is to prepare His people for their work of ministry.

Somehow we've gotten this relationship between the leaders and the people reversed, with obvious consequences. I run into pastors all the time who are practically fainting from exhaustion. They'll sigh, "Oh, Brother Hendricks, I just can't seem to motivate my people."

"What's the problem?" I ask. Often I discover that this poor fellow is wearing himself out doing ministry-related tasks that ought to belong to the people—all in the name of "serving" his congregation, of course. But hearing that, I always have the strongest urge to reply, "Friend, you're not serving them, you're crippling them! You're doing what *they* are supposed to be doing—and neglecting what God has given you to do!"

If I could change one thing about the contemporary church, it would be to enlist laity in the work of ministry. Not to do the ministers' dirty work, but to do the Lord's significant work. As Elton Trueblood put it, the first Reformation placed the Word of God back into the hands of the people of God; now we need a second Reformation that will place the *work* of God back into the hands of the people of God.

Let me give you a definition of ministry: *ministry means moving people toward Jesus Christ.* Those who are outside the household of faith need to be brought in. Those who are inside but far away from Christ need to be brought near. Those who are near need to be brought up into maturity. Ultimately, these tasks of ministry belong to the everyday Christians, not the professionals. You see, doing ministry doesn't require you to be on the payroll of a church or parachurch organization. Frankly, it probably helps if you are not, as people tend to assume that clergy are paid to be good; the rest are good for nothing!

Four episodes from the life of Elisha help to clarify our understanding of ministry. You may assume that because he was an Old Testament prophet, Elisha was on that "first team" of God's special people, and therefore is in a different category than you. Without question, Elisha was divinely appointed to a specialized task. But the principles by which he conducted his ministry apply equally to all of us.

Let's set the stage. As Elijah nears the end of his time, he and Elisha travel a circuit starting at Gilgal (just to the northeast of Jericho), east to Bethel (about ten miles north of Jerusalem), west to Jericho, and finally a few more miles west to the Jordan River (2 Kings 2:1–6).

As they pass through Jericho, they pick up an entourage of fifty prophets for whom the city was a base of operation (2:7). In those days, prophets often gathered together in collectives or schools, with one particular prophet as the leading figure. Apparently the Jericho school looked to Elijah as their guru. And why not? He had outlasted Ahab, faced down the prophets of Baal, and restored some semblance of worship of the Lord to the nation. So as he and Elisha come by, this group hastens out to the Jordan to get a front-row seat on whatever is about to happen.

They are not disappointed. First Elijah smacks the water with his cloak or mantle, and the river parts (2:8). Does that incident remind you of anything? If you know your Bible, you may recall that Joshua had previously parted the Jordan to allow the Israelites to enter the Promised Land (Joshua 3:6–17)—a miracle, by the way, that probably happened in the near vicinity of where Elijah and Elisha now cross over. So already, we can see activity that is heavily freighted with symbolism.

There will be more to come, beginning with Elisha's request to inherit a "double portion" of Elijah's spirit (2 Kings 2:9). Some have misunderstood this as a request to do twice as many miracles as Elijah, or to have twice as effective a ministry. A more likely interpretation is that Elisha was asking what any eldest son of the Israelites had a right to expect—a double portion of the family inheritance (Deuteronomy 21:17). Elijah presumably had no family, so it was only natural that he would ask Elisha, "What can I do for you before I am taken away from you?" Of course, the prophet probably had few if any material possessions, so it was also only natural that Elisha would request the one thing Elijah did possess—the authority and power of the living God.

In the next moment, a fiery chariot appears and Elijah is swept away by the Lord in a whirlwind (2 Kings 2:11). Elisha immediately recognizes that his spiritual "father" is gone for good, taken away by the hand of God. Overwhelmed—perhaps with grief, perhaps with awe—he rends his clothes, as was the custom of the day (2:12).

And now his ministry begins. The first thing he does is to pick up Elijah's mantle, which has fallen to the ground. He walks back to the east bank of the Jordan River, strikes the water, and cries, "Where now is the Lord, the God of Elijah?" (2:14). And the river parts—a clear-cut sign that Elisha has been granted his request of a double portion of Elijah's spirit.

And this is the first principle to notice in Elisha's ministry—the principle of *commission*. Elisha goes forward not on the basis of his own authority, but on the basis of God's claim on his life. That is the only basis for effective ministry. If you intend to do the work of God, you first need to make certain that God has called you to the work. Otherwise, it will be your work, not His.

This is exactly what Joshua had to learn centuries earlier. Like Elisha, Joshua was the successor to a great leader. And like Elisha, Joshua parted the Jordan. And also like Elisha (as we'll see), Joshua's first stop in Canaan was Jericho. You are probably familiar with the account of

Jericho's walls toppling after the Israelites marched around the city for seven days. But you may be unfamiliar with what happened just prior to the beginning of that siege.

Joshua was walking by himself when he encountered an armed man. Clearly startled and immediately aware that he was in enemy territory, the general drew his sword and demanded to know, "Are you for us or for our enemies?"

"Neither," the man replied, "but as commander of the army of the Lord I have now come" (Joshua 5:13–14). The heavenly visitor then commanded Joshua to take off his shoes out of reverence, "for the place where you are standing is holy" (5:15).

Some have said that the man was an angel, others believe he was an Old Testament appearance of the Lord Jesus Christ. Whatever the case, he brought Joshua to the startling realization that the battle was not to be Joshua's, but the Lord's. Joshua was not on a human conquest, he was on a divine commission. The Lord was not there to take orders, He was there to take over!

This is the fundamental premise on which all ministry must be based. If you are not convinced that what you are doing is what God wants you to do, you will either flush out when the going gets tough, or, on the other side, hijack it for your own glory when the thing succeeds. Either way, God's purposes will be poorly served.

How can you determine whether your ministry is from the Lord? First of all, by praying about it. What is it that, as Bobb Biehl asks, makes you weep with grief or pound the table with frustration? What need or problem or issue or opportunity stirs up enough passion so that you cry out to God, "Lord, someone has got to do something about this!"? Those are the matters for which God has given you a heart.

In addition, what are your gifts? What abilities has God given you that might be strategically used to address the needs about which you are praying so fervently? Every believer has been given some talent by the

Holy Spirit in order to minister in and through the body of Christ. Do you know what yours is? If so, are you putting it into practice?

Another means of determining what ministry the Lord wants you to do is to weigh the counsel of mature spiritual leaders. When you are fulfilling God's purposes for you, others will usually notice your contribution and affirm it. If they don't, you need to question whether you are really serving in your place of greatest effectiveness.

I've seen new believers come into a church and wonder, "Where do I belong in terms of service?" They try their hand here and there. Then one day, one of the pastors gets a phone call from a parent. "Hey, I don't know who that new person is that you have working with the youth group, but my teenage daughter is suddenly sky high with enthusiasm. She's reading her Bible, she's telling her friends about the Lord, she's inviting them to church—her whole attitude has changed!" Guess what—someone has found a ministry!

Not that the opinions of leaders are foolproof. I once met a fellow who had been a mid-level manager with an accounting firm. He really felt that that was where the Lord was using him—in accounting. He had opportunities to talk with people about his faith, he was leading a lunch-time Bible study, and he was helping a great many people get their financial affairs cleaned up.

As a matter of fact, he was so successful that his church noticed him. The board began talking with him about leaving his firm and becoming the administrative pastor of the church. For a while, he resisted. But then one of the men said to him, "When you finally get right with God, you'll get into full-time ministry."

Well, that did it. Obviously, he wanted to be right with God. So he left his firm, took the position at the church, and promptly became miserable. Why? Because he was out of his element (and also out of the will of God). In the church, he had little contact with non-Christians. Many of his old friendships died out. And while he was effective in handling the church's finances, he was ineffective in many other aspects of management.

Finally, he left the position at the church and went back into accounting. Result? Almost overnight he was back in business as far as doing a significant piece of work for the Lord. He also learned a valuable lesson: the advice of the well-intentioned does not always represent God's intentions. If you are experiencing a fruitful ministry already, don't jump to something else unless you are quite sure that God wants you to make a change.

This issue of how others, and especially other leaders, perceive our work brings us to the second principle to be gleaned from Elisha's ministry—the principle of *confirmation*. As soon as Elisha crossed over the Jordan, he was surrounded by the fifty prophets. I think you can appreciate why. Here was a man who had just witnessed the translation of Elijah to heaven at point-blank range. Furthermore, he had just walked across the Jordan on dry ground. No wonder the prophets exclaimed, "The spirit of Elijah is resting on Elisha!" No wonder they bowed down in a show of respect and honor (2:15).

However, the deference was not total. Somebody in the crowd had the bright idea that perhaps Elijah had not really been taken to heaven. Perhaps the whirlwind had merely dropped his body nearby. So they organized a rescue party to recover his remains (2:15). But Elisha, who knew that neither Elijah nor his body were on the planet anymore, tried to discourage this expedition. Did the prophets listen? No, "they persisted until he was too ashamed to refuse" (2:17).

This is so true to life! I preach frequently in churches across the country, and afterwards I inevitably have to endure the ritual of greeting parishioners at the rear door of the sanctuary. I call this the Glorification of the Worm Ceremony. It's not that I mind meeting the people, it's just that I usually get more praise than I deserve. "Oh, Brother Hendricks," someone will say, "that was the best sermon I've ever heard! It was just like the Apostle Paul!" Well, I doubt that.

At any rate, it's interesting that later I've had occasion to talk with some of these awed individuals about some problem they happen to be facing. They'll tell me about their troubles and then ask whether I know anything that might help them. So I'll pull out my Bible and take them to a passage of Scripture. "This is some of God's counsel on that issue," I'll explain.

But to my surprise, they often reply with something like, "Well, sure, that worked for people back in Bible times. But Dr. Hendricks, things are different now. I mean, I'm not saying the Bible isn't true. It's just . . . well, I don't think you understand." And they proceed to tell me their story all over again.

Now how is it that one minute they are putting me up on a pedestal, and the next they are putting me off as uninformed? This is exactly what the prophets of Jericho did with Elisha. They recognized that his authority and power were from the Lord—to a point. As soon as he contradicted their wishes, they demoted him. It was only when his counsel proved accurate, and a three-day search to locate Elijah's body proved fruitless, that they finally concluded, "Maybe this guy really does know what he's talking about!"

Oftentimes, God has to confirm one's ministry to dispel the doubts of others—particularly other leaders. People love to see the work of God until it works contrary to their agenda. This is what happened in the early church. The apostles started preaching the gospel and people started coming to faith. The power of God was evident. Miracles were taking place. There was excitement and enthusiasm, and everybody had the sense that "Hey, God is in this thing!"

Then one day Peter is called to Caesarea and a family of Gentiles comes to faith. *Boom!* The leaders at Jerusalem come unglued! They go into executive session and call Peter on the carpet. "You went into the house of uncircumcised (i.e., Gentile) men and ate with them?" they ask, utterly scandalized (Acts 11:2). This sense of doubt about Peter's credibility is ironic, given that all along the church has looked to him as its number one leader. Why, wasn't it Peter who had preached three thousand souls into the church (2:38–41)? Wasn't it Peter who had stared down the Jewish council (4:8–22)? Wasn't it Peter who exposed the sin of Ananias and Sapphira (5:1–11)? Now, suddenly, Peter is the man in the hot seat.

The church leaders accepted Peter's explanation of his visit to Cornelius' house. But isn't it interesting that the next time we hear about him, the Lord's angel is delivering him from prison in response to the church's prayer (12:1–17)? Just a coincidence—or a confirmation that Peter's efforts were being directed by the Lord?

I don't know what God might do to confirm the ministry He has given to you. But I do know that sooner or later, someone is going to question whether you are fulfilling God's purposes. When that happens, ask the Lord to make it evident to all concerned that He approves of your labors. By putting their doubts to rest, you will not only gain confidence, you may gain allies.

Elisha was certain that God had commissioned his ministry. He had convinced the school of prophets to that effect. Now it was time to deal with the everyday people. The text says that he had made his way to Jericho while the prophets went on a wild goose chase looking for Elijah's body. That was a sensible thing to do. It was also strategic, because Jericho was a place of need. In Joshua's day, it was the walls that had been the problem. Now it was the water.

"The men of the city said to Elisha, 'Look, our Lord, this town is well situated, as you can see, but the water is bad and the land is unproductive'" (2 Kings 2:19). This is a telling statement. In the first place, water in the Old Testament is often identified with spiritual vitality. The fact that Jericho's water was bad paralleled the fact that the spiritual life of its people—along with the rest of the nation—was stagnant, too.

In fact, it is interesting to note that Jericho had been rebuilt in the time of Ahab in direct defiance of the Lord's will. When the city was

destroyed in the time of Joshua, the Israelites razed it and Joshua pro-
nounced a curse on it: "Cursed before the Lord is the man who under-
takes to rebuild this city, Jericho: 'At the cost of his firstborn son will he
lay its foundations; at the cost of his youngest will he set up its gates'"
(Joshua 6:26).

From then on, Jericho lay desolate. People settled there, but no
attempt was made to rebuild the city. Then along came a man named
Hiel. Scripture links him to Ahab and then tells a grim tale: "Hiel of
Bethel rebuilt Jericho. He laid its foundations at the cost of his firstborn
son Abiram, and he set up its gates at the cost of his youngest son Segub,
in accordance with the word of the Lord spoken by Joshua son of Nun" (1
Kings 16:34). We don't know whether Hiel sacrificed his sons in a ritual
of idolatry, or whether they somehow died in the construction of the city.
But the point is clear: Jericho was rebuilt against the expressed intentions
of God.

No wonder its water was brackish and its lands unproductive.
The face of God was set against that city. But then Elisha arrived. Do you
know what his name means? "God is salvation." (By the way, Joshua's
name also means "salvation"—a further connection between the two
men.) Whereas Elijah ("the Lord is God") was sent to reestablish worship
of the true God, Elisha was sent to offer healing and restoration to the
land.

He began this work at Jericho by staging an object lesson. Taking
a bowl of salt, he threw it into the city's water supply with the words,
"This is what the Lord says: 'I have healed this water. Never again will it
cause death or make the land unproductive'" (2 Kings 2:21). Now I don't
pretend to know much about hydrology, the study of water, but I do know
that you don't put salt into water to make it pure. What was Elisha up to?

The answer is that, like Elijah, he was thumbing his nose at Baal,
the false god whom many of the Israelites were still worshiping, despite
the spectacular event on Mount Carmel. Baal was the god of fire, but he
was also the god of rain and vegetation. The fact that Jericho's spring was

bitter and its croplands unproductive was an embarrassment to the Baal-worshipers. Meanwhile, those who worshiped the Lord did so by bringing a daily offering of grain mixed with salt—the salt serving as a symbol of their covenant with God (Leviticus 2:13).

So by throwing salt into the water, Elisha was saying, in effect, "It's time to return to the Lord. It's time to renew the covenant. The Lord, not Baal, is the only One who can make your water—and your lives—fruitful again. Only the Lord can restore you to spiritual vitality."

It was a message of salvation. And this is the third principle to notice in Elisha's ministry—the principle of *communication*. There was a message in Elisha's ministry. He was bringing a word from the Lord, not just the goodwill of a man.

This is an important point for our day. We have so many needs around us—poverty, disease, illiteracy, starvation, addictions of every kind, poor housing, even no housing. The list goes on and on. But often we Christians find ourselves in debate and dissension over whether our first task ought to be to meet these physical needs or the underlying spiritual needs of people. I think the example of Elisha suggests an answer: we must do both. We must meet people's physical needs even as we attend to their spiritual condition, and we must never ignore people's spiritual needs as we seek to address their physical well-being.

Elisha did that. He healed the city's water—a very practical need in a climate where water was the lifeblood of the community. But in addition to serving as a civil engineer, Elisha also served as a spiritual engineer: he replenished the people's awareness of and dependence on God.

What message are you communicating in your ministry? Perhaps your service leans toward the practical—volunteering in a soup kitchen, building houses for the poor, coaching an inner-city basketball team. As you engage in these kinds of valuable activities, are you letting people know that the mainspring of your motivation is the love of Christ? Are you offering that cup of cold water *in His name*? Or are you just offering another community service that, well-intentioned as it may be, gives people no hope beyond the present?

On the other hand, are you so focused on people's souls that you overlook the fact that God created them with bodies, too? I'm familiar with many worthwhile causes for Christ that have blinders on in this regard. They take the attitude, "What good does it do to feed or house or clothe people if we're sending them to a Christless eternity?" But by that thinking, they sometimes allow the worst kinds of inhumanity to thrive. Not surprisingly, their effectiveness is compromised because their credibility is suspect. How can you convince someone that God loves him if you turn your back on his pressing and practical needs? Is that would Jesus would do?

By the way, the message of your ministry involves a lot more than developing a high-sounding mission statement. I receive documents all the time in which people and organizations espouse the most noble of intentions. But then I go and visit their operation. I talk with the people with whom they are working. I hear from their board members. I chat with their donors. I meet with their staff. And the closer I get, the more I realize that many of these ministries are not exactly what they have advertised. It's not that out-and-out deception is taking place. But they are promoting one thing while *communicating* something else. There's a vast difference.

For example, someone who supposedly set out to win the lost with an evangelistic outreach is now all caught up in the numbers and the dollars and the programs. Certainly details like these cannot be overlooked, but it becomes apparent that whatever else may be driving the effort, it is no longer a passion for reaching people with the gospel. Sooner or later, that change in focus will be communicated.

It is so easy to slight the spiritual, living as we do in a materialistic, market-driven society. That's why we occasionally need to pile up our strategic plans, our mailing lists, our pro formas, our slick brochures and lay them before God with the prayer, "Lord, you must be our strength.

Help us to stayed focused on you. Help us to keep our passion on what you have called us to. If any of the machinery of ministry is diverting us from your purposes or compromising our message, then give us the grace to lay it aside and return to a single-minded trust in your resources. Let people see that we represent Christ, not ourselves."

There's one final principle from Elisha's pattern of ministry. We don't want to miss this one! It's the principle of *confrontation*. Anytime someone engages in a significant work for God, opposition to it is just a matter of time.

For Elisha, opposition came from a group of rascals on the road to Bethel. English translations commonly call them "youths," but this was no group of boys. These were young men, perhaps false prophets of Baal, and therefore counterparts to the school of the Lord's prophets at Jericho.

By now, word of Elijah's dramatic departure had no doubt spread throughout the region. Everyone was aware that Elijah had been taken up to heaven in a whirlwind. It also seems likely that they had heard that the mantle of prophetic leadership now rested on Elisha, and that he had performed miracles at the Jordan and Jericho. So as Elisha traveled west toward Bethel, a group of several dozen young men came out to taunt him. "Go on up, you baldhead!" they cried (2 Kings 2:23). In other words, "If you're now such a great prophet, why don't you go on up to heaven like Elijah!"

But whenever one mocks the Lord's servant, he is mocking the Lord. And Scripture makes it plain that God will not be mocked! So Elisha turned and confronted them. He was not defending himself, he was defending the Lord. As the text says, he "called down a curse on them *in the name of the Lord*" (2:24, emphasis added). The result was that two wild animals mauled forty-two of the wild youths.

This passage does not give us sanction as believers to strike back when we are persecuted for righteousness' sake. Remember, our model is Christ, who, "when they hurled insults at him . . . did not retaliate; when he suffered, he made no threats. Instead, he entrusted himself to him who judges justly" (1 Peter 2:23). However, Elisha's example does encourage us to stand up for the Lord when He is mocked or maligned—just as Jesus did, for example, when the Pharisees claimed that He healed by the power of Beelzebub, or Satan (Matthew 12:22–37). Confrontation is a part of ministry.

If we are doing our job for the Lord, we will inevitably encounter opposition. Jesus said, "If they persecuted me, they will persecute you also" (John 15:20). Likewise, Paul wrote that it has been granted to us on behalf of Christ "not only to believe on him, but also to suffer for him" (Philippians 1:29). Are you prepared to pay that price? The only way you will be is if you are certain that you are fulfilling God's purposes.

When Elisha left Bethel, he traveled north to Mount Carmel (2 Kings 2:25). Scripture does not tell us why. But we can imagine that the mountaintop was quiet now. Nothing remained from Elijah's climactic encounter with the prophets of Baal—except perhaps a shallow depression where the altar had stood, and maybe a few patches of scorched earth. What was Elisha thinking as he surveyed the scene?

Perhaps this: "I have been commissioned by the Lord to carry on the ministry of Elijah. He has confirmed that calling by the demonstration of His power and the affirmation of His prophets. He has sent me to communicate His message of salvation to wayward people. And He expects me to confront every lie lifted up against Him and His Word of truth." With that settled, Elisha turned and made his way to Samaria, the capital of the kingdom, where he would carry out the bulk of his ministry.

God has a Samaria for each of us, a place of significant service. But before we go that place, we are well advised to consider four crucial elements of ministry: Are we certain of the Lord's commission? Do we need a confirmation that we are there by divine appointment? Do we have the right message to communicate? Are we prepared for confrontation? When we've answered these questions, we are ready to move people toward the Savior.

CHAPTER NINE

Mission

I suppose most people have dreams, but how many people actually turn their dreams into reality? Larry Walters is among the relatively few who have. His story is true, though you may find it hard to believe.

Larry was a truck driver, but his life-long dream was to fly. When he graduated from high school, he joined the Air Force in hopes of becoming a pilot. Unfortunately, poor eyesight disqualified him. So when he finally left the service, he had to satisfy himself with watching others fly the fighter jets that crisscrossed the skies over his backyard. As he sat there in his lawn chair, he dreamed about the magic of flying.

Then one day, Larry Walters got an idea. He went down to the local army-navy surplus store and bought a tank of helium and forty-five weather balloons. These were not your brightly colored party balloons, these were heavy-duty spheres measuring more than four feet across when fully inflated.

Back in his yard, Larry used straps to attach the balloons to his lawn chair, which was just a typical aluminum lawn chair, the kind you might have in your own back yard. He anchored the chair to the bumper of his jeep and inflated the balloons with helium. Then he packed some sandwiches and drinks and loaded a BB gun, figuring he could pop a few of the balloons when it was time to return to earth.

His preparations complete, Larry Walters sat in his chair and cut the anchoring cord. His plan was to lazily float up a couple hundred feet, spend a while enjoying the wonder of flight, then float back down to terra firma. But things didn't quite work out that way.

When Larry cut the cord, he didn't lazily float up; he shot up as if fired out of a cannon! Nor did he go up a couple hundred feet. He climbed and climbed until he finally leveled off at *eleven thousand feet!* At that height, he could hardly risk deflating any of the balloons, lest he unbalance the load and really experience flying! So he stayed up there, sailing around for fourteen hours, totally at a loss as to how to get down.

Eventually, Larry drifted into the approach corridor for Los Angeles International Airport. A Pan Am pilot radioed the tower about passing a guy in a lawn chair at eleven thousand feet with a gun in his lap. (Now there's a conversation I'd have given anything to have heard!)

LAX is right on the ocean, and you may know that at nightfall, the winds along the coast begin to change. So as dusk fell, Larry began drifting out to sea. At that point, the Navy dispatched a helicopter to rescue him. But the rescue team had a hard time getting to him, because the draft from their propeller kept pushing his home-made contraption farther and farther out. Eventually they were able to hover over him and drop a rescue line with which they gradually hauled him back to earth.

As soon as Larry hit the ground, he was arrested. But as he was being led away in handcuffs, a television reporter called out, "Mr. Walters, why'd you do it?" Larry stopped, eyed the man, and then replied nonchalantly, "A man can't just sit around."

You've got to admire someone like that! Sure, his idea was crazy. In fact, it was absolutely ludicrous! But it was also his dream, and he went after it. When you consider how many people in this world are satisfied to risk nothing, to try nothing, to imagine nothing, you begin to appreciate someone like Larry Walters. So what if things didn't work out exactly the way he planned? At least he was willing to give it an honest effort.

Elisha had something of the same adventurous spirit. He could envision what the northern kingdom of Israel would look like if it turned wholly back to the Lord, and he was willing to get involved to accomplish that vision. Thus we could say that Elisha's ministry was based on a sense of *mission*.

What do I mean by "mission"? Christians have used that word for centuries to describe the task of taking the good news of Jesus Christ the uttermost part of the world. However, when the gospel was brought to the New World, the meaning of the term shifted somewhat; instead of a task, it came to designate a temple, a building referred to as a "mission." More recently, the corporate world has discovered the term "mission," using it to describe a statement of fundamental purpose for an organization's existence.

That's not far off the mark. A mission is a charge, a guiding mandate that defines a task. In fact, "mission" derives from a word that means "to send" or "sent." Thus a person with a mission is a person with a purpose. He is out to accomplish something. He feels a sense of responsibility to fulfill that purpose, and if he is genuinely dedicated to it, it guides his actions.

Elisha was a man on a mission—no doubt a mission inherited from his mentor, the great prophet Elijah. Elijah had prevailed over the worshipers of Baal. But the nation was not yet wholly repentant. The worship of Baal may have suffered a setback, but it was far from eradicated. Therefore, the Lord raised up Elisha to complete what Elijah had started.

He had a tough job on his hands. Ahab had been succeeded by his sons, first Ahaziah, then Joram. Neither was much of an improvement over their father. And always in the background was Jezebel. So when Elisha launched his ministry, he knew he was up against spiritually bankrupt leadership.

But God has a way of breaking evil rulers. In Joram's case, he used revolt. Second Kings 3:4 explains the situation: "Now Mesha king of Moab raised sheep, and he had to supply the king of Israel with a hundred thousand lambs and with the wool of a hundred thousand rams. But after Ahab died, the king of Moab rebelled against the king of Israel."

Joram responded to this act of defiance by recruiting the southern kingdom of Judah and the kingdom of Edom, Judah's neighbor to the south, to join him in going to war against Moab. Taking a southern route around the lower end of the Dead Sea, so as to surprise their enemy, the three armies ran out of water.

Have you ever found yourself in a tight spot with one or two unbelievers? It can be an interesting situation. Faced with a genuine crisis, people who ordinarily display no fear of God can suddenly turn quite pious.

That's what Joram did after a week of going without water. "'What!' exclaimed the king of Israel. 'Has the Lord called us three kings together only to hand us over to Moab?'" (3:10).

That's rather disingenuous. Joram totally ignores God, then when he finds himself in trouble, he says, "It's the Lord who got us into this thing!" So now Joram is on a mission from God! Sounds pretty spiritual, doesn't it? But it was sheer hypocrisy. It was a backhanded way of blaming God for the situation.

Fortunately, Jehoshaphat, the king of Judah, was a genuine man of faith. So he asked, "Is there no prophet of the Lord here, that we may inquire of the Lord through him?" (3:11).

I suspect that Joram was about to change the subject when one of his officers spoke up: "Elish son of Shaphat is here. He used to pour water on the hands of Elijah" (that is, he attended to Elijah's personal needs).

At the name of Elijah, we can imagine that Joram's face took the expression of having eaten a bad oyster. Elijah had been the nemesis of Joram's father Ahab. Now someone was promoting his successor Elisha to deal with the lack of water.

But it was too late. "Jehoshaphat said, 'The word of the Lord is with him'" (3:12). So the three kings went to visit Elisha. Joram again put on his pious front, but the prophet saw right through him. However, recognizing the sincerity of Jehoshaphat, he agreed to work with the three allies.

What he told them seemed ludicrous: the kings were to have their soldiers dig trenches and then wait for God to miraculously fill them with water. It was an outrageous plan, but the kings obeyed. Sure enough, the Lord delivered on His promise: "The next morning, about the time for offering the sacrifice, there it was—water flowing from the direction of Edom! And the land was filled with water" (3:20).

The water did more than quench the allies' thirst. When the Moabites saw it, they thought it was blood and assumed that the three armies had destroyed each other. Expecting to plunder the spoils, the Moabites launched an ill-advised, poorly planned attack, and the allies were able to rout them (3:24–25). It was a complete victory for Israel, but also a complete vindication of Elisha. In fact, the account suggests three things about Elisha and the mission to which God had called him, three qualities which anyone who plans to pursue God's purposes is wise to cultivate.

The first is that Elisha was a man of *vision*. Having a vision for one's life is essential for every believer. I'm afraid churches today are full of people who have busy lifestyles, but barren lives. Their schedules are filled with activity, but devoid of accomplishment. So they wonder, "What is God's purpose for me? Why am I here on this planet?" They are lacking in a clear vision for life, and so they struggle to find meaning and purpose.

I like Bobb Biehl's observation that "focus precedes success." That's because when you have a vision for your life, you have direction. You have an idea of where you want to end up.

Have you thought about where you want to end up? I'm afraid many people haven't. Consequently, they end up nowhere. They remind me of Alice in Wonderland, who asked the Cheshire Cat which path she should take.

"That depends upon where you want to go," replied the Cheshire Cat.

"Oh, it really doesn't matter where I go," said Alice.

"Then it doesn't matter which path you choose," answered the Cheshire Cat.

As Christians, it matters very much where we end up. Presumably we want to end up in God's will. Therefore, we cannot afford to disregard His intentions for our lives. We need to do whatever we can to line up our plans with His plan. In fact, I have yet to find a successful, fulfilled individual who did not have a focus, a direction, a vision for his life.

So how does one come by that? Does it involve some sort of mystical, ethereal process? Not at all. Anyone can develop at least some sense of vision by evaluating the resources that God has given him. By resources, I mean three things in particular: talents, motivation, and opportunities.

Has it ever occurred to you that every talent, every skill, every ability you possess has been given you by God? Some of these are evident from the womb, others you seem to acquire along the way. But all of them are actually God's gifts to you, to accomplish His purposes. For example, God has given me the ability to teach. However, he has *not* given me the ability to fix cars. So that makes His will fairly apparent: He wants me to teach, not fix cars.

This way of looking at oneself would seem fairly obvious, wouldn't it? Yet I'm amazed at how many people slight the wonderful talents God has given them and try to do things for which He has given them no talent. For instance, I'll meet a guy who is convinced that he's supposed to be selling insurance. The problem is, he can't sell worth a dime! So he's frustrating himself, his customers, his employer, and everyone else. Meanwhile, he's got talent like you wouldn't believe for sprucing up lawns and gardens. So why doesn't he get out of the insurance business and apply himself at landscaping?

In addition to abilities, God has given each of us the motivation to do a particular thing. My passion in life is teaching, which makes sense, given that I have ability in that regard. As a result, I teach at a seminary. Someone else may be motivated to persuade, and matches that motivation with his ability to write, resulting in highly influential articles and editorials. Another person may be motivated to render aid to other people. Applying that through his skills in management and planning, he works as a project coordinator for a relief agency.

What is the motivational passion that drives you? To compete? To acquire? To assist? To improve? There are scores of possibilities. Whatever your fundamental drive is, you need to identify it. You also need to recognize it as a resource from God's hand. He has given you that drive so that you have the energy to carry out His purposes.

Of course, talent and motivation require opportunity. So as you evaluate your life, ask yourself: What are my options? Where can I best use my abilities and motivation? You have to be realistic in answering that. You may have genuine talent and passion for, say, performance, but unless you've paid a lot of dues, it is unlikely you will star in a Hollywood motion picture anytime soon. That's not a realistic opportunity. But acting as the emcee for your Sunday school class's Christmas banquet may be.

If you will start with the opportunities close at hand, you will often find that greater opportunities surface fairly quickly. But if you ignore the immediate possibilities, hoping that something better will come along, it probably won't. Perhaps that's because opportunities are given us by God. He wants us to be faithful in the little things before He hands us something greater.

Once you have some idea of what your abilities, motivation, and opportunities are, you can bring focus and direction to your life by pulling those elements together into a statement of vision or purpose. Here are a few examples of what I'm talking about:

"I am here to love God and reveal His love to others— especially those who are hurting."

"God put me here to make the world a better place for other people."

"I exist to help others succeed."

"My purpose for living is to serve God by using all of my abilities to their maximum potential in a way that improves the lives of others."

These vision statements were written by a counselor, a carpenter, a financial planner, and a salesman, respectively. As you can see, they are not long or complicated, but they are specific and clear. They also are based on a clear cut awareness of God's resources. As a result, they summarize the strategic direction of these people's lives.

Imagine how helpful it would be to have a vision statement like that for your life. Why not take some time right now to reflect on your own life, and start working toward a statement that might summarize God's purpose for you?

William Jennings Bryan was a great turn-of-the-century preacher, lawyer, and statesman who ran for the presidency of the United States three times. From his background on a Nebraska farm, he grew up to become the dominant political force of his era. In fact, the American press dubbed him the Peerless Leader. Asked on one occasion how he was able to come so far, Bryan remarked, "Destiny is not a matter of chance, it is a matter of choice. Not something to be waited for, it is something to be achieved." That's what mission is about. A man with a mission—like Elisha—doesn't wait for destiny to catch up with him. He develops a vision and then goes about achieving it.

But vision alone is not enough. It's got to be paired with *integrity*. Vision without integrity is not mission—it's manipulation. Elisha was a man of integrity. He was upright, honest, and sincere. When the three kings began wondering who could help them out of their dire straits, the first name that came to their advisors' minds was Elisha. He was known to be a straightforward person with a close walk with God. In fact, even though Joram probably expected the prophet to tell him something he didn't want to hear, he agreed to consult him because he knew he would get an honest response.

Integrity is an essential component to any mission. There has to be a confidence that the person accomplishing the mission can be trusted, that his word is true. Otherwise, he lacks credibility.

A United States senator (who shall remain nameless) was running for president several years ago when someone challenged his educational credentials. Taking the query as a personal insult, the senator replied, "I think I have a much higher IQ than you do," and boasted that he had attended law school on a full academic scholarship. He also claimed to have finished in the top half of his class, to have been designated the "outstanding student" in the political science department, and to have graduated with three degrees.

But it's a dangerous thing to make extravagant claims to a press that can be ruthless in checking out the details. It was only a matter of time before it came out that the senator had received only a half-scholarship, and that was based on need, not academic merit. Furthermore, he had finished 76th out of 85 in the class, did not win the political science award, and graduated with only one degree, not three. Quipped one pundit, "In light of those revelations, doesn't the IQ statement seem a but dubious, too?" Needless to say, that politician's presidential aspirations were quickly dashed. Who wants a liar in the White House?

How different Daniel was! If you are looking for a model of integrity, I recommend spending time with this man. The account of his life can be found in the Old Testament book that bears his name. Like the senator, Daniel was a powerful, highly placed government official. In fact, he led a distinguished career spanning some eighty years under several kings and two empires. The remarkable thing is that even though Daniel's entire life was spent working for pagan idolators, he remained faithful to the Lord.

An incident late in Daniel's life bears testimony to his unimpeachable integrity. The Babylonian empire in which Daniel had served was taken over by the Persians. However, the Persian king, Darius, retained Daniel as one of his top three administrators. It was a wise decision, because Daniel performed brilliantly. In fact, he was so competent that Darius made plans to promote him. In effect, Daniel would become prime minister over the whole empire.

As you might imagine, this plan did not sit well with the other officials in Darius' administration. Not only did they have their own designs on wresting power for themselves, they knew that with Daniel in charge, their policies of dishonesty and greed would be held in check. So they decided to bring Daniel down. But how?

Scripture records that they made a thorough background check—and you can bet they dug deeply! They pulled his file and examined his dossier. They rifled through his papers. They interviewed his former associates. They looked at his checkbook, his bank statements, his credit card slips. They subpoenaed his telephone records. They even checked out his report cards, all the way back to kindergarten! But despite all of that, they came up empty-handed, Unlike the case with the senator, "they could find no corruption in him, because he was trustworthy and neither corrupt nor negligent" (Daniel 6:4).

Daniel was a man of unimpeachable integrity. In fact, there was only one way that Daniel's detractors could think of to derail his nomination: "We will never find any basis for charges against this man Daniel unless it has something to do with the law of his God" (6:5). That statement tells you everything you need to know about Daniel's character. He could not be bought. He could not be compromised. He could only be "accused" of obeying God.

Could that be said of you? I'm finding that many who have big plans for changing the world would do well to start by changing themselves. Obviously, we need people with vision. But if I had to choose between vision and integrity, I would pick integrity every time. The person who is honest and upright may or may not go far in this world, but Proverbs 11:3 promises that his life will have direction. By contrast, the person who has a big scheme but no character is dangerous. He is liable to lead others off course because his own moral compass is defective.

If you want to develop integrity, I suggest that you recruit a handful of other people to whom you can hold yourself accountable. Get together every week and ask yourselves the tough questions: How is your walk with the Lord? How is your marriage? What compromises have you been tempted to make at work? How is money affecting your life? How is your thought life? If you will commit to being brutally honest about matters like these, I guarantee that you will start seeing integrity in your life.

There's one final element to Elisha's sense of mission: in addition to vision and integrity, Elisha was a man of *passion*. That is, he felt a strong conviction about the things to which God had called him.

When the three kings came knocking on his door, Elisha was faced with a bit of a quandary. Here was Joram, trying to pass himself off as God's servant. "It was the Lord who called us three kings together," he glibly said to the prophet (2 Kings 3:13). Of course, Elisha knew that was a crock. Joram was just as wicked as his father had been. Aside from one minor cosmetic change, he was continuing in the idolatrous ways of his forebears (3:2–3).

So Elisha had nothing to say to him. In fact, he asked him, "What do we have to do with each other? Go to the prophets of your father and the prophets of your mother" (3:13). In other words, "Don't waste my time!"

Still, while Elisha might have been content to let Joram and his army perish in the desert, he was committed to a deeper purpose. Remember what it was? Elisha was called to bring a message of salvation. He had brought that message to Jericho (2:19–22). Now it was his duty to bring it to Joram and his allies. So the prophet agreed to inquire of the Lord on their behalf.

What is your passion, your fundamental commitment? What conviction are you determined to honor, even if it means overlooking someone's pretense and overriding your distaste to even be in their presence? I'm afraid that many of us are passionate, but not about the things that really matter. Some of us can get all lathered up about sports, but we're snoring like a buzz saw when it comes to our own spiritual condition. We knock ourselves out to advance our business, but when it comes to advancing the cause of Christ, we're missing in action.

Chuck Colson tells of speaking on the campus of a secular university. He was talking about his commitment to Christ, and mentioned that he was willing, if necessary, to die on behalf of the Savior. A young man in the crowd angrily interrupted, shouting, "C'mon, Colson! Nothing is worth dying for!"

To which Colson replied, "If there is nothing you are willing to die for, then I submit you have nothing to live for."

That kind of passionate commitment is becoming harder to find among believers in America. But Christians elsewhere understand that following Christ may involve sacrifice, and even death. In 1991, an Ethiopian man named Wandaro went home to the Lord. Wandaro was twenty years old when missionaries arrived in his village. They had a book that told about the Creator, and said people should worship Him, not Satan, as Wandaro and his people did.

Within a few weeks of hearing this message, Wandaro publicly announced, "I renounce Satan to follow Jesus." He was baptized, and immediately he asked to be taught to read, so that he could learn more from the missionaries' book.

It was clear from the outset that Wandaro's love for the Saviour had become the driving force of his life. When his infant son was dying of a fever, the witch doctor implored him to make sacrifices to demons. But Wandaro refused. "I love my baby boy," he replied, "but I will not sacrifice to the demons again."

The boy died, and the villagers went into their customary rituals of mourning. But as they were wailing and cutting themselves in diabolical fury, Wandaro rushed among them, shouting, "Stop! I miss my child, but God has given me peace in the face of death. I believe that my child is safe in the arms of Jesus."

As a result of Wandaro's testimony, people began to pay attention to the message about Christ. But few were prepared to accept it. Then, in 1936, the Italian army seized the country, and within a few months, the missionaries were expelled. They left behind forty-eight believers.

That was forty-eight too many for the invaders and their Ethiopian collaborators. A campaign of intense persecution began. Christians were arrested and beaten. Their property was destroyed. Their churches were torched. Yet, as often happens when Satan turns up the heat on God's people, evangelism thrived, and the persecution only served to bring more people to faith.

Finally, an official named Dogesa decided to make an example of Wandaro. After destroying the Christian's church building, Dogesa had Wandaro arrested, tied up, and beaten in the center of the village. "Now you will give up this religion!" Dogesa said.

"Never!" Wandaro cried.

Dogesa then instructed the crowd, "Do not listen to Wandaro. See how he is bound? Do not go to his church. It is torn down."

But Dogesa had misjudged his man. Wandaro began shouting to those standing by, "This rope is not the final judgment—it is only placed on me by man! Believe on the Lord Jesus Christ and you will be freed from sin!"

At that, Dogesa ordered his men to beat Wandaro with a whip. During the flogging, he taunted the stalwart believer by saying, "The foreigners have all gone. They aren't here to help you. Give up!"

But even that did not sway Wandaro's faith. "I am not serving the missionaries," he shot back, "but the God who sent them. He will strengthen me!"

And the Lord did. The next day, five men beat Wandaro for three hours, determined to break him and win the day. Finally, when he refused to bend, they locked him up in a bamboo cage. He survived, but he remained in custody for an entire year.

Then one day he was released. Do you know what he did first? He gathered the other Christians and went to Dogesa's field to help harvest his oppressor's crops!

In 1942, missionaries were allowed to reenter Ethiopia. Imagine their amazement when they learned that God had multiplied their original forty-eight converts into a church of *ten thousand believers!* A beaming Wandaro met his old friends. "Welcome! Welcome!" he shouted. "This is like heaven! God has sent you back. We need you to teach the new believers. See how many there are now? But they are untaught."

May I ask a question? It may prove disturbing: How many people have been compelled to trust Christ as the result of watching our lives? Somehow, I doubt that many of us could place the number at ten thousand! But let's not get sidetracked by numbers; the issue is *passion.* What is there in our lives that we are deeply and fundamentally committed to, so much that it drives our choices and behaviors and, under the right circumstances, even leads to sacrifice? If we want to be people of mission, then we must be people of passion. With Martin Luther we must be able to declare, "Here I stand! I can do no other."

CHAPTER TEN

Maturity

One of American Christianity's greatest men of faith during the colonial period was David Brainerd. Struck by the callousness with which he saw the European transplants treating Native Americans, Brainerd decided at the age of nineteen to go and preach the Gospel to the Indians.

Everyone told him his plan was ludicrous. They pointed out that he could not speak the native languages. He would only meet with hostility, they warned, because these were animistic peoples whom, they assumed, were naturally suspicious of missionaries. His talents would be wasted and his health surely ruined by attempting to live among these pagans.

But Brainerd believed in a big God who could overcome any obstacle—as long as His servants were willing to obey Him.

Consequently, he shrugged off the naysayers and set off to encounter the Indian. During the next nine years, he brought an estimated ten thousand tribespeople to faith in Christ. Then suddenly, at age twenty-eight, his ministry was cut short by a fatal bout of consumption, brought on by a combination of overwork and the harsh weather endured in his travels.

Yet while Brainerd died in the prime of his youth, he left behind an impressive legacy of spiritual maturity. His diary reveals a life marked by prayer, an unshakeable faith in God's plan and provision, and a willingness to suffer for the cause of Christ. The text is one that we who name the name of Christ today would do well to explore as a manifesto on maturity.

In contrast to Brainerd, I find that too many of us have allowed our sense of the spiritual to be corrupted by the culture. For example, here's brother Smith, highly successful in the business world, highly regarded as a leader in the community, lives in a spacious mansion, drives a late-model import. However, while brother Smith has made a profession of faith, he's made zero progression in the faith. He's still as immature as the day he accepted Christ—and it shows up in nearly everything he does. But does that stop his church from placing him in leadership? By no means! He's been voted onto the board. He's been put on committees. He is given prominence in front of the people.

Meanwhile, over here is brother Schmatzkopf. He's not nearly as impressive. He works a night job, leads a quiet life, lives in a two-room shack, and drives a beat-up clunker. At church, people smile and shake his hand politely, saying, "So good to see you, brother!" But it's clear they sort of look right past him—which is a shame, because brother Schmatzkopf amounts to a spiritual giant. He's got a highly developed prayer life. He's a man of unblemished integrity. He regularly seeks ways to communicate his faith. He knows what his spiritual gift is and employs it. Most importantly, he has a deep, abiding walk with the Savior. Yet when it comes to the oversight of the Lord's church, he is consistently passed over.

Does this scenario sound at all familiar? If so, it's because we need to rethink our understanding of the Christian life. God doesn't equate success with spirituality. He knows that Christians tend to grow more as a result of suffering than success. He recognizes our need for trial, not just triumph. In fact, His Word is filled with accounts of those who discovered His grace in the midst of the grind. Sometimes their trials were the bitter fruit of poor choices they had made. Nevertheless, God proved faithful, and it was when they hit bottom that they finally learned the sufficiency of His resources—a lesson that usually marked a whole new departure in terms of their spiritual development.

Even Jesus learned obedience through the things that He suffered (Hebrews 5:8). But we tend to forget that. Can you imagine if Jesus' earthly ministry had been carried out today? Some of us would be saying, "Wow, Lord, you really blew it! You never should have tapped that Judas fellow to be one of your followers. He obviously didn't have what it takes. And you really should have worked more closely with the political structure. You know, a little better job of lobbying, and things might have turned out differently. You ended up getting killed, and, well, doesn't that suggest a major lack of planning and judgment?"

It's so good that the Lord's ways are not our ways! However, He wants our ways to *become* His ways, and that involves a process of spiritual maturation. Elisha can serve as our model in this regard. He was man of faith in a society mired in faithlessness. I am often asked, what does spiritual maturity look like? A couple of encounters between Elisha and two Israelite women suggest three principles.

1. Mature Faith Remains Loyal in the Face of Apostasy

Second Kings 4 begins with a widow's desperate plea. Whenever you come across a widow in Scripture, mark it well. There's a strong probability that the writer is pointing to *systemic* injustice. You see, God has a special concern for widows. It's not just that He feels compassion for a woman's emotional loss, though obviously He does. But in that day, a woman without a husband was a woman without any means of material support. God had made provision for that when He gave His people the Law. But invariably, when the people turned away from God, their apostasy showed up in the institutions of society, which allowed people to disregard the needs and rights of widows and orphans.

That's what was going on in Elisha's day. One of the prophets had died, leaving behind a wife, two boys, and a pile of debt. The widow had nothing with which to pay the debt, so the creditor was threatening to settle it by means that were perfectly legal for that day—seizing the two boys as slaves. With time running out, the widow turned for help to her late husband's former master, Elisha (2 Kings 4:1).

It was a wise decision, because Elisha was willing to stand for God against the prevailing winds of the culture. Is that your commitment? When everyone else around you is caving in to compromise, are you holding fast to righteousness? That's never easy, but it's absolutely essential.

Of course, many of us, when faced with the moral and spiritual breakdown of an apostate society throw up our hands in despair, crying, "It's no use! What can one person do?" But Elisha was like his predecessor Elijah. He knew that one plus God always makes a majority. Here, there were *two* plus God—Elisha and the widow. Their combined faith in a faithful God would be all that was required.

Legally, there was nothing Elisha could do. The creditor was within his rights. Furthermore, as far as we know, Elisha had no means of repaying the woman's debt. But he did have compassion, and that was the starting point for his involvement. "How can I help you?" he asked the widow (4:2). A simple question, but perhaps the most significant. It indicated a *willingness* to heed her circumstances.

Again, this willingness was counter-cultural. Jesus pointed out that there were many widows at that point in Israel's history (Luke 4:25). Apparently most of them were in straits that were just as dire as this woman's, if not more so. Yet the society was not only turning its back on them, it was taking advantage of them.

Do you know any cases of that going on today? If not, I suggest that you go out and buy a newspaper. Or go talk with your pastor. He can probably give you a long list of cases where people are in desperate circumstances—and no one seems to care.

God scored Israel for ignoring the cries of its poor (for example, Amos 2:6–7; 5:11–12). Eventually, He judged the nation by bringing the Assyrians to destroy their land. What, then ought our response to be when the New Testament asks us, "If anyone has material possessions and sees his brother in need but has no pity on him, how can the love of God be in him? Dear children, let us not love with words or tongue but with actions and in truth" (1 John 3:17–18).

We cannot meet every need. There may be little we can do to meet any need. But lack of ability need not translate into a lack of availability. Elisha asked, "How can I help?" He was willing to pay attention, even if he could afford nothing else.

However, notice that the prophet matched his compassion with creativity: "What do you have in your house?" he asked (2 Kings 4:2). I think there's a connection. If you are willing to help, you will often find a way to help. But your mind will never be inventive if your heart is basically insensitive.

The woman motioned with empty hands to show the prophet her empty house. "Your servant has nothing here at all," she said. But then, perhaps glancing toward the cold ashes of her cooking fire, she added, "except a little oil" (4:2).

You may wish to underline that little word "except" in your Bible. It appears puny, but it is extremely potent! Just think of all the places in Scripture where there was no hope and no resources *except* for something or someone. For instance, when God told Israel to go up and possess the Promised Land at Kadesh Barnea, everyone became fearful of the giants in Canaan and rebelled—*except* Caleb and Joshua, who eventually entered the land (Numbers 14:30). When Gideon went against the Midianites, he had no army—*except* for three hundred men (Judges 7:7–8). When David went against Goliath, he was unarmed—*except* for his slingshot and five smooth stones (1 Samuel 17:40). When the disciples rummaged through a crowd of five thousand to see how much food there was, they came up emptyhanded—*except* for a little boy's five loaves of bread and two fish (John 6:8).

The lesson would appear to be that "except" is never a reason to doubt God. That's what makes Him an exceptional God! He often turns that which we dismiss as insignificant into the means by which He answers our prayers. So the question is not, how much do we have for God to work with, but how much are we *trusting* God to work with?

One of our seminary students told me that he and his wife once needed $142. They had carefully examined their budget and determined $142 was the absolute minimum they had to have to get through the month. At the time, it seemed like a huge amount of money, and they only had five days in which to get it. So they began praying and asking God for $142.

The next day they received a rebate check for $70 from a life insurance policy they had cancelled two years earlier. The insurance company had been trying to track them down all that time, and had finally found them and sent the check a few days earlier—before this couple had ever prayed about their need. The day after that, two more small rebate checks from some grocery purchases, one for $5 and the other for $2, arrived in the mail. Two days later, the husband got a belated birthday card. Inside was a check for $15. Finally, they were down to the last day, but were still $50 short. They knew there would be no mail, as it was a Sunday. But that morning at church, someone handed them an envelope, saying, "We just felt you could use this." It held a check for $50.

The checks totalled $142. They had prayed in faith, and God had responded. Later, the young man told me, "Prof, I learned my lesson on that one—I should have asked for a million!" God delights in responding to the prayers of those who have faith in Him.

Elisha, anticipating that He was about to set this woman up in the oil business, instructed her to beg and borrow every last piece of crockery she could lay her hands on. "Don't ask for just a few!" he told her rather pointedly (4:3).

I admire this woman's faith. Having asked the prophet for help, she went out and did what he told her to do. I wish more people had that willingness to respond to God's instructions. I get so weary sometimes of hearing about someone with a need who goes to a pastor or some other spiritual leader and asks for help. After making the need a matter of some prayer, the advisor comes back and tells the person something specific and practical that he can do. It may not be everything, but it's a place to start.

Yet how does this individual respond? By acting in faith? No, by sitting on a chamber pot of doubt! "All he did was tell me to pray," the person will complain. "All he did was tell me to go and apply for temporary work. I've already done that about fifty times."

When I hear that, I have the strongest urge to say, "Friend, did it ever occur to you that God may be telling you that you need more prayer before He can meet your need? Or that it will be on the fifty-first time you go out on a temporary assignment that you will land that job you are so desperately seeking? You think God just ignored this person's prayers on your behalf?"

God *always* responds to faith exercised through obedience. I have a pastor friend who recently was visiting our nation's capital. He told me that as he was being driven by the Senate Office Building, the Holy Spirit suddenly told him to stop, get out, and pray. Now you have to understand that this man is about as conservative as you can get. So he felt more than a little awkward with the idea of asking the driver to pull over. After all, what was he going to say—that God had told him to do so?

But then he thought, "The Lord is calling you." So he had his friend stop, and he got out. But that was just the start of his adventure. Now what was he supposed to do? He wandered into the Senate Office Building, feeling sort of sheepish and out of place, and beginning to wonder whether he had not made a rather foolish mistake. But eventually he found himself outside the office of one of his own senators.

"What am I doing here, Lord?" he prayed silently.

The answer came back: "I want you to pray."

"What! Here? In the hallway of one of our nation's most powerful buildings? For a man I didn't vote for and don't particularly like?"

But the word came again: "Pray for him."

Now it just so happened that this senator was in deep trouble with the Senate ethics committee. So the pastor began to pray. Not in a disruptive way. He just bowed his head and began to lift up the senator and his situation before the Lord.

After a few minutes, some Senate aides came walking by. "Do you need some help, sir?" they asked.

"Uh, no," my friend replied. "I'm just here . . . well . . . I'm here to pray for the senator."

The aides gave him some of those looks that say, "We don't know where you've escaped from, but we're not about to stand around and find out!" So they hurried into the senator's office.

A few minutes later, a senior aide came out. "Can I ask what you're doing?" he said somewhat officiously.

Thoroughly embarrassed, the pastor mumbled, "I'm, I'm praying for the senator. I know he's got an ethics committee hearing tomorrow, and I just felt I should pray for him."

He expected the aide to call Security, but instead he just stared. Then he turned and went back into the office. But a few moments later, he reappeared. "Would you come with me, please?"

This time, it was the pastor who stared. "Who? Me?"

But he followed the aide into the office, where, after finding a small room and closing the door, the aide told him, "I'm a Christian, too, and we could really use your prayers. It's going to be a tough day tomorrow."

So they prayed together, right there in the senator's office. Then, suddenly, the door opened and the senator himself walked in, trailed by a bevy of reporters.

"We were just praying for you," the aide told his boss. "This man showed up here and said God told him to pray for you."

At that, the room got very quiet. The reporters were dumbfounded. But the senator took the pastor by the arm and led him into his private office. When they were alone, his eyes filled with tears and he asked my friend to start praying again.

A little while later, he was back on the street. "So, do you mind telling me where you were?" the driver of the car asked.

"No, but you'd never believe me!" my friend replied.

I don't know exactly how God used that man's prayers in the life of the senator, but I do know this: God always honors obedient faith. The question is not whether He can be trusted to do what He has committed, but whether you can be trusted to do what He has commanded. That's the process by which you develop maturity in your walk with Christ.

2. Mature Faith Remains Content In the Face of Greed

Next to being widowed, childlessness was probably the worst fate that could befall a woman in the ancient world. Not only was barrenness considered a curse, it was almost always blamed on the woman. So it's interesting that the next incident recorded in Elisha's ministry involved a barren woman from Shunem (2 Kings 4:8, 14). Whereas the first woman feared that her two boys would be taken away, this woman had never had children to begin with.

Like widowhood, childlessness was feared not only for emotional reasons, but practical ones as well. Children, particularly sons, carried on a family's name, and, among the Israelites, inherited its lands, thereby keeping them in the family. When a son came of age and his father passed on, it was his duty to take care of his mother. When a daughter married, she often saw to it that her husband's family cared for her mother if there were no sons to assume the responsibility. But if there were neither sons, daughters, nor any other relatives, a widow usually faced a bleak outlook—especially if the society had abandoned God's laws, as Israel largely had.

However, the prospect of living in destitution was not a concern for the woman of Shunem, known as a Shunammite. She was fortunate to be married to a well-to-do man. Furthermore, she was secure among her relatives. As she told Elisha, "I have a home among my own people" (4:13). Thus when her husband died—and he soon would, as he was advanced in years—her material needs would be taken care of, even though she was without children (4:14).

The remarkable thing about this woman was her generosity. Somehow she encountered Elisha, probably while he was visiting the region in connection with his prophetic role. Shunem was only about three miles north of Jezreel, a vineyard region where the royal family had lands (1 Kings 21:1, 15; 2 Kings 8:29). Whatever the circumstances, the Shunammite invited Elisha to share a meal in her home. This visit led to numerous others, suggesting that she was a person of faith, though curiously the text does not say one way or the other.

But it does tell us that the Shunammite recognized Elisha as a holy man of God, so she arranged to furnish a room for him (2 Kings 4:9). This act reveals much about the Shunammite's heart. It tells us that she was tender toward the things of God, and also that she was generous with her resources.

Have you ever known someone like that? I'm glad to say that I have. I could mention any number of people whom I have personally seen share their resources to further the Lord's work and assist those engaged in it as vocational Christian workers. They have been generous not just with money, but, like the Shunammite, with their possessions—their houses and guest houses, their cabins and lake homes, their cars, their boats, their planes, their equipment. Somehow these dear people of God, some of whom control considerable wealth, hold their worldly goods with open hands, always ready to make them available to the Lord.

"Well, I could be generous, too, if I had that kind of wealth," you may be thinking. If so, consider this. My home state of Texas recently organized a biweekly lottery, and it's now the number one lottery in the country. Do you know what the number one rationale people give for playing the Texas Lottery? If they win, they'll do something charitable with the money. That's what they claim! They'll donate to an orphanage, endow a school, give money to their church. They have all kinds of fantasies about how generous they *would* be, if only they had the means.

You may have had similar dreams. But there's a simple test of whether your intentions are honest: how generous are you *right now*? You see, it's easy to fantasize about giving to charity after winning the big one. That's like spending someone else's money. But the question is, what are you doing with *your* money, the money you have *right now*? If you are not already generous, then no amount of money is going to change your heart for the better. Indeed, it may change it for the worse.

The Shunammite had an honest heart. In fact, she demonstrated a great deal of spiritual maturity when Elisha decided one day to thank her for all her kindnesses. Through his servant Gehazi, he said to her, "You have gone to all this trouble for us. Now what can be done for you?" (4:12).

Elisha intended to bless her, but his offer was actually a test of her character. Open-ended gifts always are. Remember God's offer to Solomon? "The Lord appeared to Solomon . . . in a dream, and God said,

'Ask for whatever you want me to give you'" (1 Kings 3:5). Imagine God handing you a blank check! Just fill in the amount. Whatever you want—the riches of heaven stand at your disposal. That offer was also a test of character—and Solomon passed the test with flying colors by asking for wisdom and a discerning heart (3:9). He showed that his affections were wholly devoted to the Lord.

The Shunammite showed similar strength of character by essentially telling Elisha, "Thank you, but I have all I need—and I'm content with that" (2 Kings 4:13). In fact, this woman was content with what she did *not* have—children! When Elisha told her that God was going to give her a son, she objected and tried to decline the offer (4:16).

I marvel at that kind of maturity. And, if you will pardon the expression, I "covet" it for God's people today, particularly those of us who live in the West and have resources that most people throughout most of history and most of the world today could hardly even imagine. We have been materially blessed beyond measure. Many of us have so much junk, we can't even fit it all into our homes. Somebody had to invent a whole new industry called "mini-storage" to provide enough room to warehouse our extra stuff.

So when we discover that Jesus Christ had more to say about money than about heaven and hell *combined*, we need to pay attention. He's talking to us! When we discover that Scripture in general has more verses on money than on any other topic, we need to pay attention. The Holy Spirit is talking to us! When the apostle Paul wrote to pastor Timothy to "command those who are rich in this present world" (1 Timothy 6:17), he was thinking of us—rich Christians.

What was Paul's charge? Command them "not to be arrogant nor to put their hope in wealth, which is so uncertain, but to put their hope in God, who richly provides us with everything for our enjoyment. Command them to do good, to be rich in good deeds, and to be generous and willing to share" (6:17–18).

How do we develop that open-handed generosity, living as we do in a society saturated with greed? Only by cultivating intimacy with Jesus Christ, so that we are thoroughly satisfied both with what He gives us, and also with what He doesn't. "Godliness with contentment is great gain. For we brought nothing into the world, and we can take nothing out of it. But if we have food and clothing, we will be content with that" (6:6–8).

I'll never forget going on a short-term mission trip to a village of dirt-poor peasants in Mexico. The pastor of the church there was living in a tiny, one-room adobe house. Many of the men in his congregation had no jobs. The children—those who were dressed—were dressed in rags, and were playing in bare feet. Believe it or not, their only toy was an old oil filter tied to a string.

When it was time for dinner, my hosts took the metal mesh seat from an old lawn chair they had found in the dump, and placed it as a grill over the fire. Then they brought out the scrawniest chicken I think I've ever seen in my life, and roasted it down to the size of a pigeon.

Finally, when we were ready to eat, the pastor quieted everyone and began to pray, using these words, "Oh, Lord, you have given us so much. . . ."

I about lost my appetite right there—and it wasn't because of the food! I was utterly stunned by the contentment in this man's life. I thought, "Given you so much? You've got to be kidding! How can you say that?"

Then the Lord said to me, "Howie, it's all a matter of perspective."

A person of mature faith is content with what God gives him— and doesn't give him.

3. Mature Faith Remains Confident in the Face of Circumstances

The Shunammite did not really want the boy God promised her (2 Kings 4:16). Oh, I think she wanted a child—desperately. But I think she had lived for so long as a barren woman that she had come to grips with her barrenness. Now, all of a sudden, God's promise upset her equilibrium.

But bearing a child helped to build this woman's faith. Children often do, though we parents have an uncanny way of overlooking that. Have you ever had a young couple at your church ask everyone to pray that God would give them children? He answers their prayers, and sure enough, six weeks after the kid is born, the couple is back, only now they are praying, "Lord, why did you give us children?"

However, the Shunammite was tested by the ultimate ordeal, the one that every parent fears—the death of her only son (4:18–21). So she saddled her donkey (which, by the way, was the equivalent of a Lexus in that day; only royalty and the very wealthy rode on donkeys), and went to Elisha, who happened to be up on Mount Carmel. The text indicates that she was in bitter distress and grief, but her words suggest outrage, too: "Did I ask you for a son, my Lord?" she said to Elisha. "Didn't I tell you, 'Don't raise my hopes'?" (4:28).

I can't even imagine what Elisha must have felt at that moment. He had tried to honor this gracious woman with the blessing of a child. Now his kindness seemed more of a curse. He had hurt the very person he had wanted to help.

But Elisha's response is a casebook study in crisis management. Whatever he said and did next was going to prove determinative in helping this woman cope with her tragedy. First he sent Gehazi to the boy with his staff—a symbol of his spiritual authority. But he himself remained with the woman—and said nothing. Have you discovered the power of presence and the solace of silence? Oftentimes when people are hurting, they need us to close our mouths and open our arms. That's what Elisha did. He stayed with the woman while Gehazi hurried ahead.

But as he followed behind the Shunammite's donkey on that long road down the mountain toward Shunem—probably the same road on which Elijah had outrun Ahab's chariot (1 Kings 18:46)—you can bet that he and the Lord had quite a conversation! Scripture does not record what he said, but it does tell us that when he arrived back at his guest room, Elisha immediately went to work in a way that shows he fully expected the Lord to perform a miracle (2 Kings 4:32–35). This suggests that just as the Shunammite had said, in effect, "Elisha, you got me into this," so Elisha in turn told the Lord, "Lord, you got me into this," but also added, "now I trust you to see us through it."

There is no indication that Elisha doubted for a moment that God would raise the boy from the dead. After all, he knew that God had already done that in the time of Elijah (1 Kings 17:17–24). Now it was Elisha's turn to demonstrate God's power, not only to the woman, but to everyone who would hear of this miracle.

That includes us. The Holy Spirit preserved the memory of this incident in Scripture for our instruction. What does He want to teach us? That when God gives us a gift or a responsibility, we are not allowed to give it back. He expects us to see it through.

Notice that when the child died, the Shunammite "went up and laid him on the bed of the man of God, then shut the door and went out" (4:21). Why did she do that? Because she expected a miracle? Probably not. I think she did it out of anger. She had provided a furnished room for Elisha, and he had returned the favor by giving her a son—over her objections. Now the child had died, fulfilling her worst fears. So she left the boy's body in the prophet's room, as if to say, "Here, take back your 'gift'! It has only ruined my life!"

Have you ever felt that way? Sure you have! Sometimes you'd just as soon return God's "gift" of that spouse who seems so difficult. Sometimes you'd just as soon be rid of that career for which your God-given talents suit you so perfectly. Some people wish they had never been given the money, or the fame, or the power, or the position that God has chosen to "bless" them with. With great privilege comes great responsibility, and sometimes, as in the Shunammite's case, great pain as well.

But God was not ready to take the boy back. He wanted him to grow up under this woman. That was a part of His plan. This boy would someday cause kings to fear the Lord (see 2 Kings 8:1–6).

I suspect that most of us have prayed for God to heal someone, but the person nevertheless died. Or, like the student mentioned earlier, we have implored God for money to come in, but it never did. Does that mean God has failed us? Certainly not! It means that He has purposes that we do not know, perhaps cannot know. Our challenge is to trust that whatever He gives us—be it life or death, health or illness, riches or poverty, pleasure or pain—somehow figures into His plan. And it is *His* plan, not ours. We only experience our small part in that plan. He assures us that our part, along with everyone else's, is all working together for good, but He has not chosen to reveal the entirety of what He's up to—not yet, anyway.

So we walk by faith, not by sight. To some, that feels like planting one's feet firmly in mid-air. But God is not asking us to step off a cliff, He is asking us to place our hope in Him. Those who do discover an interesting thing: over time, they are no longer climbing mountains, but soaring over them, held aloft by the wind of God's Spirit. That wind is available to any of us at any moment. But the birds who make the most of it are the ones who develop their wings—the fully mature wings of faith.

CHAPTER ELEVEN

Modeling

I was driving my car along a crowded freeway a number of years ago, frantically trying to get to an appointment. The road was a mess because construction had reduced the thoroughfare to one lane of traffic. There in front of me was some guy taking his sweet time, puttering along as if the rest of us had all day! There was absolutely no way to get around him, and my blood pressure started going through the roof.

"Come on, you joker!" I shouted in frustration, and gave the steering wheel a little whack for good measure.

My son, who was just a boy at the time, was sitting in the passenger's seat beside me, playing with his toy car. A couple days later we were stuck in traffic again, only this time I wasn't in such a rush. But as we were waiting for someone in front of us to move, I heard my boy sing out, "Come on, you joker!" and give his little car a whack.

That's when I felt the Lord giving me a bit of a whack! "Hey, Hendricks, don't you see? As a parent, you are a model for your children—for better or for worse. Monkey see, monkey do!" It was a wake-up call that I desperately needed. There I was, thoroughly wrapped up in my own tension and hurry, completely oblivious to my role as a father. It never dawned on me that my boy was paying attention as I let off a little steam. I assumed he was as self-absorbed as I was. But he was watching me like a hawk!

I'm not suggesting that anyone try to put on a front of good behavior for his or her children. They'll see right through that. But we need to remember that we are setting a pattern for them to follow. That's what proves so disturbing to me today—when my grown children do the very things that I used to do, and wish I hadn't. Every time I see that, I think, "Now where do you suppose they learned that?"

One of the most important things Jesus did was to serve as a model for His disciples. In the short span of three and a half years, he took a group of common men and taught them to live an uncommon life. It was not just His talks that transformed them—though His talks were vital. But it was His walk that proved determinative. He *showed* them how to pray, how to battle temptation, how to deal with those who opposed them, how to take a stand for the truth. He certainly preached forgiveness, but when a woman was caught in adultery, He put feet on that sermon by the way He dealt with her. Likewise, He preached love for one's enemies, but it was by dying on the cross, crying out, "Father, forgive them, for they know not what they do," that He demonstrated God's love.

It was not just for the Twelve that Jesus modeled godliness. He is the divine pattern for believers today, as well. In turn, you and I are models to those around us—for better or for worse. Unbelievers are watching us, to see whether Christ makes any difference in our attitudes and actions. Other believers are watching us, to see whether Christ makes any difference in our values and commitments. Our families are watching us, to see whether Christ makes any difference in our relationships. As noted, our children especially are watching us, to see whether Christ makes any difference in how we love them and show them how to live. Does that kind of visibility give you cause to pause, as it does me?

A pastor opened his church to the neighborhood ladies society, arranging with the custodian to set them up in the building's fellowship hall. A week or so later, he and the youth minister were working in the back of the church, moving some boxes. It was a tedious task, and before long, they had turned it into a little competition. At first, it was just a challenge to see who could move boxes more quickly. But then things escalated into a silly game of cops and robbers. Pretty soon, these two grown men were chasing each other through the halls of the church, firing imaginary pistols at each other and making the appropriate noises.

At the height of their play, they went running down the main hallway, burst into the fellowship hall, somersaulted across the floor, and ended up in firing positions. The pastor shouted, "Freeze, turkey!" About that time, he noticed that he and his partner were not alone. Eight elderly ladies, sitting in a circle of folding chairs, sat staring at two men firing their fingers at each other.

Desperate to redeem the situation, the pastor stood up, "holstered" his "weapon," looked at the ladies, and said, "Sermon preparation! I'm, uh, going to be preaching on spiritual warfare soon. Thought it might help to engage in a little role play." The ladies smiled and nodded, but it was clear they were wondering whether this sort of thing went on all the time.

You never know when someone is watching. In fact, as a Christian you have to assume that someone is *always* watching. You are always modeling the faith—for better or for worse. That's why Paul wrote, "Be very careful, then, how you live—not as unwise but as wise" (Ephesians 5:15). The aim is to live "blameless and pure, children of God without fault in a crooked and depraved generation, in which you shine like stars in the universe as you hold out the word of life" (Philippians 2:15–16).

Elisha modeled godliness in a wise, discerning way. Remember that he himself had an outstanding pattern to follow in his predecessor, Elijah. Now it was Elisha's turn to shine like a star in a crooked and depraved generation. Notice four areas in which he modeled what it means to be God's person.

1. Holiness

Elisha was known as a holy man among his own people, and his reputation spread to the pagans of his day. These included the Arameans, who controlled the lands around Damascus, to the north of Israel. Aram frequently attacked Israel during this period, nibbling away at its territory and carrying away plunder and captives.

The general who led these raids was named Naaman. The Bible tells us that he was valiant in battle, but somehow he contracted leprosy (2 Kings 5:1). The term leprosy describes a variety of skin conditions, one of which was incurable, and usually fatal. In fact, the Israelites believed that only God could heal someone from leprosy (5:7). This dreaded disease now struck the pagan commander, and, like most people in that circumstance, he began casting about for a cure. In the providence of God, Naaman's wife had acquired a servant girl from among the Israelite captives, and it was she who recommended that he see Elisha (5:2).

I am intrigued by two things upon reading this account. The first is the smart and timely suggestion of the little girl. She was awake to opportunity. She could not help Naaman herself, but she knew someone who could, and she spoke up. You and I are in much the same position. All around us are people with an incurable disease of the spirit—sin. We cannot help them ourselves, but we can lead them to the One who brings healing to the human soul. And even if we feel inadequate to do that, we can at least introduce them to some other believer who can.

The other thing to note is that this little girl's recommendation speaks volumes about Elisha's reputation and credibility. It was not just kings and other prophets who recognized him as a man of God. Even little girls in the border towns of northern Israel knew that he stood for God. There is not the slightest bit of doubt or hesitation in the servant girl's suggestion: "If only my master would see the prophet who is in Samaria! He would cure him of his leprosy" (5:3).

Imagine having a reputation like that! Imagine the unbelievers in your office or neighborhood coming across someone struggling with spiritual questions and needs, and saying, "I can't help you, but I know someone at work, or down the street, who can," and they send that individual to you. *That's* a model of righteousness!

I believe God wants us to cultivate that kind of reputation—a reputation for holiness. Otherwise, He is left without a witness in a world of darkness.

When Charles Spurgeon, the great nineteenth-century preacher at All Souls Church in London, began his ministry, a famous atheist informed his friends that he was going to listen to Spurgeon preach.

"Why?" his friends asked incredulously. "You don't believe a thing that man says!"

"No, I don't," the atheist agreed, "but *he* does."

Even an unbeliever can appreciate the fervor and faith of a person totally sold out to God. That's why Peter urged the early church, "Live such good lives among the pagans that, though they accuse you of doing wrong, they may see your good deeds and glorify God" (1 Peter 2:12). That's what Elisha did; he set an example of holiness.

Does the prospect of leading a holy life put you off? Are you inclined to say, "Forget it, I'll never live up to that standard"? If so, then you are ready to experience grace. For the fact is, none of us can live up to God's perfect standard of holiness. If we could, Christ would not have had to die. But He did die—on our behalf—because only He was holy enough to satisfy God's expectations. Thanks to Him, we can now stand before a holy God, by grace. And because we have that standing, we are called to pursue a holy lifestyle, to become like our Savior.

Let me suggest three practical implications of that truth. The first one has to do with obedience: holy living means living wholly for the Lord. One reason people had so much respect for Elisha was because he did whatever God asked him to do. Christians are called to that same single-minded devotion to the Lord. Peter wrote, "As obedient children, do not conform to the evil desires you had when you lived in ignorance. But just as he who called you is holy, so be holy in all you do; for it is written: 'Be holy, because I am holy'" (1 Peter 1:15–16).

A second principle is that living with holiness means living with a reverence for God. Peter went on, "Since you call on a Father who judges each man's work impartially, live your lives as strangers here in reverent fear" (1:17). Do you show respect for the Almighty? Many today do not. They make Him the butt of jokes. They drag His name into profanity. They mock the things that are dear to His heart. But those who fear God honor Him as Creator, Lord, and ultimately Judge.

Finally, pursuing holiness involves self-control. "Dear friends," Peter wrote, "I urge you, as aliens and strangers in the world, to abstain from sinful desires, which wage war against your soul" (2:11). We are living in occupied territory. Our enemy, the evil one, is always ready to ambush us with things that entice our sinful desires. So Peter says, pay attention! Be on your guard. Exercise self-control!

How about you? Are your words pure? Can people tell you are a follower of Christ by the things that come out of your mouth? I don't mean using a bunch of Christian clichés. Is God glorified in your speech?

How about your thought life? You may not be able to control every tempting thought that enters your mind, but you can control how much time you spend pondering it. Are you feeding your mind garbage and filth—or the pure milk of God's Word and meat of God's truth?

How about your sex life? Scripture is clear that holiness goes hand in hand with sexual purity, which involves self-control: "It is God's will that you should be holy; that you should avoid sexual immorality;

that each of you should learn to control his own body in a way that is holy and honorable, not in passionate lust like the heathen, who do not know God" (1 Thessalonians 4:3–5).

The great Scottish evangelist Robert Murray McCheyne said, "A holy man is a mighty weapon in the hands of God." Is that what you aspire to be, a weapon of God? If so, you can rest assured you will also become a target of Satan. He will do anything to bring you down. Therefore, Peter warned us, "Be self-controlled and alert. Your enemy the devil prowls around like a roaring lion looking for someone to devour. Resist him, standing firm in the faith. . . . And the God of grace . . . will himself restore you and make you strong, firm and steadfast" (1 Peter 5:8–10).

2. Heart

One time I was watching some children at a playground. One little girl accidentally bumped into a boy from behind, knocking him to the ground and causing him to skin his knee. Guess what he did? He immediately jumped up, ran after the girl, and shoved her to the ground, where she burst into tears. Not surprising, is it? The most natural thing in the world is to try to hurt someone who has hurt us. When we see that spontaneous reaction in children, we begin to realize that retaliation is the human way.

But it is not God's way. As we consider options for dealing with our personal enemies, Jesus challenges us to love them and pray for them (Matthew 5:44).

I find that hard to do. That's how I know when God's love is operating through me—when I act with a love that I ordinarily would not have. For instance, one time an acquaintance said some things about me that were not exactly true. When I confronted him with it, he denied everything. "I never said that!" he claimed, somewhat defensively. "You must be getting bad information."

But I had good reason to suspect just the opposite, and I felt deeply hurt. Later, someone called me to ask my opinion of this fellow.

He was being considered for a ministry position for which he was clearly qualified. Naturally, I thought, "Here's my chance. I can finally pay him back."

But then the Lord brought this verse to mind: "When they hurled insults at Him, He did not retaliate; when He suffered, He made no threats. Instead, He entrusted Himself to Him who judges justly" (1 Peter 2:23). So now I had a choice to make. Would I retaliate against this man by torpedoing his career opportunity with a bad report, or would I play it fair, out of obedience to God?

I decided to play it fair. Understand, I didn't *want* to say anything positive. That wasn't my natural response. But God had changed my heart. He was living His supernatural life through me as I informed the inquirer that I was sure this man was qualified for the position; however, he and I had had some personal clashes, so a less biased perspective could probably be had from someone else.

In a world full of conflict and tension, God's people are called to model tenderheartedness. That's what Elisha did. When Naaman heard that there was a prophet in Israel who could heal him of leprosy, he immediately asked the king of Aram for a leave of absence. "By all means, go," the king replied, and sent him off with a letter to the king of Israel (presumably Joram), and gifts to secure his cooperation (2 Kings 5:4–6).

Naturally, the Israelite king was suspicious. But Elisha's heart was attuned to this pagan warrior's desperation. Instead of taking the attitude, "Good! I hope he dies. That'll be one less Aramean to worry about," the prophet welcomed him, and even saw an opportunity for God to be glorified, saying, "Have the man come to me and he will know that there is a prophet in Israel" (5:8).

Do you know anyone who you can never imagine turning to God in repentance? A friend of mine had a buddy like that. The two of them used to sail together, and my fried, who was a Christian, regarded the other guy as a total reprobate. He figured that never in a million years would this man humble himself before God. "Howie," he told me, "one time Charlie had a can of beer sitting in the cockpit, when he turned around and knocked it to the deck. When he saw the entire can spilling out, he ripped off some choice cuss words and the remark, 'I'd rather see a church burn!'"

But then something happened. Charlie ran into some severe problems in his relationships. He began to look at my friend, the Christian, and noticed something different about his relationships. That started him wondering, and they got to talking about what makes life worth living. Eventually Charlie started doing a little Bible study, and before long, that "reprobate" became a redeemed child of God! But the transformation in Charlie's life was matched by the transformation in my friend's perspective. "I would never have believed it (that Charlie could have come to faith) unless I'd seen it with his own eyes!" he told me.

A similar situation occurred with Naaman. At first, he rejected Elisha's instructions to go and bathe in the Jordan River (5:10–12). But his aides convinced him to reconsider. When he did as Elisha said, his health was miraculously restored. Notice the response: "Now I know that there is no God in all the world except in Israel. . . . Your servant will never again make burnt offering and sacrifices to any other god but the Lord" (5:15, 17).

No one expected that—no one but Elisha. Everyone else made an assumption: hardened soldier, devoted enemy of Israel, idol worshiper—he'll never crack! But Elisha knew that the Lord can change hearts. Remember how Elijah temporarily turned Ahab's heart to repentance (1 Kings 21:17–29)? As Elijah's servant, Elisha was probably standing by and witnessed that transformation first-hand. If Ahab, who was completely hostile toward God, could change, why not Naaman, who was at least seeking some sort of answer to his problem?

If you want to be like Elisha and develop a heart for others, let me suggest that you start by praying for individuals by name. Jesus commanded us to pray for our enemies, but how many of us put that into practice? We are more likely to ask God to save us *from* our enemies, than to save our enemies.

During the Gulf War between Iraq and the United States and its allies, a group of Iraqi Christians was huddled together in Baghdad. Do you know what they were doing as the bombs were raining down on their city? Praying! Praying for the leaders of the United States—and for Saddam Hussein! Somehow, I think Elisha would have admired that.

But be careful when you pray for an enemy—you might end up liking him! You might end up as his friend! That's what happened to Dolphus Weary of Mendenhall, Mississippi. After God led him to assume the leadership of a ministry started there by John Perkins, Dolphus began to pray for the leaders of Mendenhall, a small town about forty miles south of Jackson. Like many Southern towns, Mendenhall had always been racially segregated. Dolphus was black. The leaders of the town were white. Some were known to be members of the Ku Klux Klan. So when it came to prayer, Dolphus had his work cut out for him!

But he began lifting up the names of those in power—the mayor, the town council, the county commissioners, the major employers. Then one day at a speaking engagement, he was shocked when one of these leaders approached him and asked to learn more about Dolphus' work at The Mendenhall Ministries. This man was a prominent Klansman, and Dolphus naturally felt reticent to even converse with him. But in the course of conversation, he discovered that God had been working in this man's life. In time, the Klansman repented of his racism and turned his life over to the Lord. He began to take a keen interest in what God was doing through The Mendenhall Ministries, and eventually came on the board!

Our world is filled with people like that man—people who are angry, confused, hurting, lonely. They need the life-changing love of Jesus Christ. The problem is, their needs and troubles often cause those of us who could introduce them to Christ to pull away in disgust. That's why prayer is so important. It changes us more than anyone else.

Having prayed, our next step in cultivating a heart for people is to get involved with people. There's a classic "Peanuts" cartoon in which Lucy shouts, "I love humanity! It's people I can't stand!" Not to make anyone feel uncomfortable, but . . . isn't that the attitude of a lot of Christians? We get all shook up about the pitiful souls over in Booga Booga Land—people we've never met and probably never will meet this side of heaven. Meanwhile, we can't be bothered with the guy down the street who is only a heartbeat away from a Christless eternity. We see him all the time mowing his lawn, washing his car, playing with his kids. We even wave and act neighborly. But we never make the effort to get next to him and find out whether he has any interest in hearing the Gospel.

If we want to model tenderheartedness, we've got to take the initiative and find out what people's needs are. And when we find out, we've got to step in and do what we can to meet them.

My friend Allan Emery, for many years a director of Service Master Industries, tells of accompanying his parents on a cross-country train ride from Chicago to Phoenix in 1937. During the ride, Allan learned that one of the porters was in great pain due to an ingrown toenail that had become infected. When Allan's father learned of this, he asked the porter whether he could help. Eventually, the man agreed to let Allan's father lance the infection, clean it out, and wrap a bandage around it to keep it clean.

After this "operation," the porter came through the observation car, where Allan happened to be sitting. He had tears running down his cheeks, and made it as far as the men's lounge before he slumped down in one of the leather benches and began bawling like a baby. Greatly concerned, Allan went over to see what was the matter.

"Are you crying because your toe hurts?" Allan asked him.

"No, it is because of your daddy," the porter replied, and broke down all over again.

Finally Allan was able to get the story out of him. "While he was dressing my toe," the man began, "your daddy asked me if I loved the Lord Jesus. I told him my mother did but that I did not believe as she did. Then he told me that Jesus loved me and had died for me. As I saw your daddy carefully bandaging my foot, I saw a love that was Jesus' love and I knew I could believe it. We got down on our knees and we prayed and, now, I know I am important to Jesus and that he loves me."

And with that, he burst into tears all over again. But they were tears of unabashed joy, and in the midst of them he blubbered out, "You know, boy, kindness can make you cry."

The body of Christ could stand to produce a lot more tears like that!

3. Humility

Elisha was a holy man and a tenderhearted man. He was also a humble man. After Naaman dipped himself in the Jordan seven times and came out with a cover-girl complexion (2 Kings 5:14), he naturally felt indebted to Elisha. So he tried to press a gift on the prophet, but Elisha refused.

I interpret that as a sign of humility. It was not that Elisha didn't have needs. Nor was he too proud to accept anyone's largess. Remember how he gladly accepted the Shunammite's gift of a furnished room (4:8–11)? But notice his response to Naaman: "As surely as the Lord lives, whom I serve, I will not accept a thing" (5:16).

Elisha was far more concerned about the Lord's reputation than he was about his own. He was far more interested in God being worshiped than in his getting wealthy. He wanted Naaman to go back to Aram and tell everyone there that the Lord had healed him as gift of His grace, absolutely free of charge. That way, the idolatrous gods of the Arameans would be put to shame, along with their priests, to whom people forked over enormous sums in hopes of extracting a few favors.

I can just hear Naaman now: "You won't believe it! This prophet down in Samaria looks me over, sends me down to this dinky river where I take a swim, and guess what—I come out healed! Absolutely healed! Skin as soft as a baby's! But the real clincher is, this guy doesn't charge me a thing! Not one measly shekel! Said it was all the Lord's doing. Said if I wanted to show my gratitude, I could worship the Lord for the rest of my life. You can bet that's what I'll be doing!"

Elisha's example is so refreshing. He bent over backward to get out of the way, so that Naaman could see who had really healed him. He didn't want to eclipse the Lord. How different he was from his foolish servant Gehazi, who, tragically, used this incident as a pretext to advance his own interests (5:19–27). Likewise, how different he was from so many today, who claim to stand for Jesus Christ, but the more you listen to them, the more you hear about them and their concerns, and the less you hear about Jesus Christ and His concerns. Perhaps they could stand a dose of John the Baptist's attitude: "He must increase, but I must decrease" (John 3:30).

One of the most important things you can do as a model is to be humble. Leonard Bernstein, the master composer and orchestra conductor, was once asked to name the instrument for which he had the hardest time finding qualified players. Without skipping a beat, Bernstein replied, "Second fiddle!"

It's easy to find people to take the starring roles, to play the solos, to garner the attention. But who is willing to play second fiddle? That's what it means to "shine like a star" in a crooked and perverse generation. In a world where everyone wants to be top dog, it's actually the humble servant who stands out. That's why Paul instructed the Philippians, "Do nothing out of selfish ambition or vain conceit, but in humility consider others better than yourselves. Each of you should look not only to your own interests, but also to the interests of others. Your attitude should be the same as that of Christ Jesus" (Philippians 2:3–5).

A few pages ago I related a story about a porter who was led to Christ by Allan Emery's father. As you can see, his father was a man who paid attention to the "little people" in life. This led to a lasting friendship with another porter who worked on a different train. On one occasion, that porter asked Mr. Emery if he could ask him a question. Emery was only too happy to oblige. So after the train arrived at its final stop and all the passengers had disembarked, the porter came and told the following story:

"There were two boys in my family. My mother worked very hard to teach us all she could and to see that we had the best education available at that time. I was a good student. When I had graduated from high school, I went to work as a railroad waiter and then I got this job. My whole desire was to help my mother and fulfill her wish that I go to college and become a preacher. She wanted her life to count by seeing her son a preacher.

"Well, I saved my money, and while I was doing this, my younger brother went in a different direction. He drank and partied and nearly killed himself by living for the devil. About the time I was accepted at college, my brother was converted. He decided he wanted to preach. He had nothing, so he asked me to provide for his education. I was so happy to see this great change in his life, I agreed and today my brother is a nationally known preacher. You may have heard him on the radio. He has led thousands to Christ.

"So, you see, I couldn't go into the ministry and I am too old now. Mr. Emery, my question is this: Do you suppose the Lord will give me some credit for the souls my brother led to him?"

Allan Emery says that his father was so deeply moved recounting this story to his family that night that he nearly broke down. Everyone knew what his answer would have been, and the biblical principle behind it is expressed in the verse, "The share of the man who stayed with the supplies is to be the same as that of him who went down to the battle. All will share alike" (2 Samuel 30:24).

Are you willing to carry bags, if that's what God has for you? Are you willing to work behind the scenes, away from the "front lines," in order for God's purposes to be accomplished? God is not looking for more stars, He's looking for more servants. He may have you serve, like Elisha, right where the battle is fiercest. Or He may have you serve, like the little servant girl, in the backwaters of His plan. But what matters is not so much where you serve, but *Who* you serve, and with what spirit. As Jim Elliott put it so well, "They also serve who only stand and wait."

(The two stories from Allan Emery are contained in his book, *A Turtle on a Fencepost*, Word Books, 1979).

CHAPTER TWELVE

Multiply

There once was an Englishman named Charles Peace—an ironic name, because Peace was not a peaceful man, but a contentious one. Violent, thieving, brawling, he was a career criminal who respected the laws of neither God nor man. Eventually the authorities caught up with him, and he was tried and condemned to death by hanging at Armley Jail in Leeds.

On the morning of his execution, a contingent of prison officials met at Peace's cell to take him on his final walk to the gallows. Among them was a sleepy prison chaplain whose job it was to prepare the condemned man's soul (such as it was) for the hereafter. As the group began its solemn death march, this parson began mumbling and yawning his way through a series of unintelligible recitals.

Suddenly he felt a tap on his shoulder. "What are you reading?"

someone was asking. He turned to find it was Mr. Peace.

"The Consolations of Religion," he replied

"Do you believe what you are reading?" inquired the prisoner.

"Well, yes, I guess I do."

Peace stared at the chaplain, stunned. Here he was, going to his death, knowing that his earthly deeds utterly condemned him before the ultimate Judge, and this clergymen was mouthing words about heaven and hell as if it were a boring chore. He said to the parson, "Sir, I do not share your faith. But if I did—if I believed what you say you believe—then although England were covered with broken glass from coast to coast, I would crawl the length and breadth of it on hand and knee, and think the pain worthwhile, just to save a single soul from this eternal hell of which you speak."

What a profound statement! Charles Peace may have lacked faith, but he was hardly lacking in insight. Even as an unbeliever, he instinctively recognized that if the Gospel is true, every Christian is morally bound to proclaim it at every opportunity—certainly when one stands with his neck in the noose as a condemned criminal!

Christ has called us to this very task. He wants His people to make a difference—a difference not only in this world, but in the world to come. There can be no greater legacy.

Paul captured the essence of this mandate when he wrote to his young protégé Timothy, "The things you have heard me say in the presence of many witnesses entrust to reliable men who will also be qualified to teach others" (2 Timothy 2:2). He was describing a ministry of multiplication. Every time you impact the spiritual life of another individual, you set in motion a process that ideally never ends. Just as you build that person up in Christ, so he is to communicate Christ to others. Therefore, the question becomes, who are you pouring your life into, so that they, in turn, have something to offer someone else?

A judge in a juvenile court was battling a massive crime wave. Kid after kid was hauled before him, most of them from a particular neighborhood in the inner city. Finally, exasperated with the monotonous onslaught of criminal activity, he asked one young offender, "Where did you learn to do this stuff?"

The adolescent replied, "Rocko taught me."

When the next case came up, the judge repeated the question: "Who taught you to steal?"

The answer was the same: "Rocko did."

Over the next three days, the judge found thirty-three juvenile delinquents who had picked up their criminal skills from the nefarious Rocko, whoever he was. Realizing that this person was the key to cutting the crime rate, the judge instructed the district attorney to find him and bring him in. Two days later, Rocko stood before the bench.

"Well, what do you have to say for yourself?" the judge demanded. "I've got a jail full of minors whose lives you've corrupted. How could you do such a thing?"

"Eddie taught me," the young man replied.

There's a lesson there for the church! How many of us decry the fact that our communities are being overrun by gangs? We demand tougher law enforcement and more cops on the street. But I'm afraid that strategy hopelessly misdiagnoses the situation. If defeating gangs were merely an issue of raw force, stiffer sentences and increased firepower might do the job.

But we are up against something far more powerful and effective—the power of life-on-life relationships. In a perverted but potent way, gangs do what the community of faith ought to have been doing all along—multiplying themselves by using the influence of personal relationships to affect the attitudes and behavior of juveniles in a deep and lasting way. Gangs provide an alternative to kids who have no purpose, no hope, and in many cases no family.

By the way, who was the Gospel addressed to? Those who had no purpose, no hope, and in many cases no family! Check it out; it's right there in the New Testament. To a large extent, those were the people most quickly attracted to the upstart movement of Christ-followers.

Imagine: that movement began with a handful of weak-kneed people in an upstairs room in Jerusalem, and by the end of the first century, it was turning the known world upside down—despite opposition so extraordinary that it makes the American justice system's war on crime look downright friendly. How did the early Christians accomplish that? Obviously by the power of the Holy Spirit. But their *strategy* involved a ministry of multiplication—one person influencing another, who in turn influenced others.

Elisha used much the same approach. Obviously, he lived in a different era, and was called to a different task—namely, acting as God's official spokesman to the northern kingdom of Israel. Thus, we cannot draw a direct parallel between him and the first Christians. His aim was to speak the Word rather than to spread the gospel. Still, he did spread godliness, and we catch a glimpse of his method by Scripture's references to "the company of the prophets" (2 Kings 2:3, 5, etc.).

We encountered these prophetic schools earlier when we looked at Elijah's dramatic departure in the chariot of the Lord. Apparently in those days, prophets were clustered in groups scattered throughout Israel and Judah. The school at Jericho seems to have been one of the more prominent. The text suggests that it included at least fifty men (2:17), and perhaps more. A modern seminary with fifty faculty members would be a large school, so the Jericho group was a significant community.

Each of these schools looked to a main prophet for guidance, inspiration, and probably validation of their work. We don't know exactly how this relationship worked, but Scripture contains a number of important clues. For one thing, the prophets often followed their leaders in their travels, either individually, as Elisha did with Elijah (1 Kings 19:21), or in groups (2 Kings 2:3, 5, 7).

Does this sound familiar? It should. It was the strategy of Jesus. He recruited a group of followers, who became his *disciples* ("learners"), and He their *Rabbi* ("teacher"). Interestingly, the prophet Isaiah, who lived about a century after Elijah and Elisha, also referred to the prophets surrounding him as his "disciples" (Isaiah 8:16). So when we read that a company of prophets met regularly with Elisha (2 Kings 4:38; 6:1), we have good reason to assume that it was a teaching situation.

Furthermore, we can conclude that Elisha must have been a good teacher, because the group appears to have grown in numbers under his ministry. As any teacher can tell you, that's a good sign that one is communicating effectively. Elisha must have been, because one day the school ran out of room: "The company of the prophets said to Elisha, 'Look, the place where we meet with you is too small for us. Let us go to the Jordan, where each of us can get a pole; and let us build there a place for us to live' And he said, 'Go'" (6:1–2).

With that, a building program got underway. And while most Bible readers probably skip over this incident, it was actually the high-water mark of Israel's spiritual life during that period. Think back a few years to the quiet conversation between Elijah and the Lord outside the cave on Mount Horeb. Do you remember the prophet's complaint? "The Israelites have rejected your covenant, broken down your altars, and put your prophets to death with the sword. I am the only one left, and now they are trying to kill me too" (1 Kings 19:10, 14).

Of course, Elijah was not alone. There were still seven thousand people left who remained faithful to the Lord. But most of them were hiding in caves. Nevertheless, within the space of a few decades, we find a school dedicated to God's Word going up on the banks of the Jordan River. That's impressive: from a cave to a campus! What accounts for this relatively spectacular rebound? Ultimately, the credit goes to the Lord. But two figures feature prominently in the biblical account: Elijah and

Elisha. Significantly, both were committed to a ministry of multiplication.

Do you want to be involved in making that kind of impact on your generation? Then I suggest you follow the same strategy. Get involved in life-on-life relationships with a handful of other people. Don't worry about numbers—worry about *names*. That is, pay attention to individual persons. Find out what their needs are, their hopes, their God-given talents and abilities. Begin praying with them and for them, that God would work in these areas of their lives, to give them purpose, meaning, direction, and effective service for Him. We've already looked at some practical aspects of mentoring and modeling, so I won't repeat those principles here.

But I would point out that if you want to influence the lives of others, sooner or later you are going to run into some opposition. Satan likes things just the way they are, so he's not going to stand by passively while believers start claiming territory for the cause of Christ. He's going to wage war against your efforts—primarily in the spiritual domain. Let me suggest two areas where you can expect a diabolical counteroffensive, based on the experience of Elisha—two points of attack as you attempt to take a stand for God.

Anger

The backdrop to our study is a siege. Earlier we looked at Naaman, the commander of the army of Aram, Israel's neighbor to the northeast. Throughout the time of Elijah and Elisha, the Arameans regularly raided the Israelites, and vice versa. But this time, Ben-Hadad, king of Aram, was going for broke. Instead of just plundering a few border towns, he sent a major force to capture Israel's capital city of Samaria.

Doing so would not be easy. Samaria stood on a hill above the plains, and, like nearly all major cities of the day, it was walled. The only effective means of taking such a city was to besiege it—to surround it with troops and cut it off from all outside supply. This was the approach of Ben-Hadad (2 Kings 6:24).

Sieges could last months or even years. They invariably caused untold hardship, both physical and psychological, on the unfortunate citizens of the city under attack. In Samaria, the food eventually ran out. The text describes how dire this situation was by reporting that a donkey's head, considered unclean by the Israelites, was worth a fortune. Even a bowl of seed pods, which may have been extracted from bird droppings, sold for five shekels (6:25). Obviously, the situation was desperate.

So desperate that the citizens were turning to cannibalism. We read the tragic account of two women who made a grim pact with each other—to kill and eat their two infant sons. However, after slaughtering and eating the one boy, the mother of the other reneged (6:29).

If this sickening tale provokes disgust in us, it prompted outrage from the Israelite king: "When the king heard the woman's words, he tore his robes" (6:30), following the customary way of expressing intense emotion. But notice on whom he vented his anger: "He said, 'May God deal with me, be it ever so severely, if the head of Elisha son of Shaphat remains on his shoulders today!'" (6:31).

Elisha? Why would the king be mad at Elisha? Because Elisha stood for the Lord. Furthermore, he was an easy target. You see, the king knew in his heart of hearts that the fate hanging over his city was not caused by the Arameans; they were only the effective cause. The sufficient cause was the nation's apostasy and the king's own corruption and idolatry. The heathen at the gate merely represented God's judgment on these sins. That's why the king finally admitted, "This disaster is from the Lord" (6:33).

Elisha had no doubt warned the king of impending judgment. Now that it was falling, the king took the all too common path of rulers in trouble: he ignored the message and called for the death of the messenger. What he should have done was fall on his face in repentance, asking God to forgive the nation of its sins. Instead, he got angry at the one man who could explain why things were falling apart.

A former student of mine went through a similar situation as Elisha. He was called to be the pastor of a large church on the West Coast, a church that had gone through a series of pastors in short order. It didn't take this new man long to identify the problem. A small clique of deacons had the church in a stranglehold. Unloving and inflexible, they were bent on pushing their agenda. Finally the pastor went to the board of elders, laid out the problem, and called for change. But instead of thanking him, they became angry. How dare he come in and start telling them what was wrong? A vote was taken and the pastor was let go. Predictably, that church has continued to languish—another case of ignoring the message and killing the messenger.

Elisha gives us a model for dealing with such opposition. He stayed calm and stuck to the truth. When the king's men came calling, he was meeting with the elders of the city. He didn't panic, he didn't run, he just locked his door and waited for the king himself (6:32).

By the way, I wonder what Elisha and the elders were doing. Do you suppose they might have been doing what the king ought to have been doing—holding a prayer meeting to humble themselves before God and implore Him to deliver the city? Scripture does not tell us, but based on everything we know about the prophet, this seems like a reasonable inference. It would certainly be characteristic of someone intent on multiplying his faith.

Unbelief

But faith always demands a response, and given an opportunity to trust God, the king and his advisors responded with doubt and disbelief. Convinced that the Lord had given up on him, the king was ready to give up on the Lord. "Why should I wait for the Lord any longer?" he asked (6:33). Apparently he was ready to turn to other means to save his city—perhaps to burn sacrifices to his idols, perhaps to sue for peace.

Have you ever been in that situation? Maybe you've been hanging in there with your marriage, your job, or your church, trying to hold on in the midst of problems and conflicts. You've been praying and waiting for God. But then something happens that brings you to the end of your patience, and you decide, "It's no use. God isn't going to do anything. I'll just have to handle this myself."

Such is the resignation to doubt. We find numerous examples of this in Scripture. For instance, God promised Abraham and Sarah a son, but when Sarah grew old and had not yet born any children, she came up with a Plan B: according to the custom of the day, she gave her servant Haggar to Abraham to raise up an heir through her (Genesis 15:15:4; 16:1–4). Likewise, when the Israelites settled into the Promised Land, they waited for the Lord to establish a king. But when their leader, the judge Samuel, grew old, no king was in sight. So they demanded that he draft Saul as their sovereign (1 Samuel 8:1–10:26).

I don't know exactly why God sometimes takes us to the end of ourselves before He acts, but I do know that trading faith for unbelief always leads to disaster. Paul itemizes some of these breakdowns in Israel's history in 1 Corinthians 10. Then he warns us that we, too, are susceptible to failing the tests of our faith. Our challenge is to hold onto the fact that "God is faithful; he will not let you be tempted (or tested) beyond what you can bear. But when you are tempted, he will also provide a way out so that you can stand up under it" (1 Corinthians 10:13).

It seems uncanny, but the "way out" often doesn't appear until just the moment when one is ready to throw in the towel. That's what happened in Samaria. With the situation so desperate that mothers were turning into cannibals and the king into a skeptic, Elisha brings a prophetic word from the Lord: in twenty-four hours, the situation will be completely reversed. Food will be so plentiful that it will practically be given away. Note that the prophet punctuated this promise with the imprimatur, "This is what the Lord says" (2 Kings 7:1). That made it official. God had spoken!

Has God spoken to believers today? Of course He has, particularly in terms of multiplying our faith. When Peter declared that Jesus was the Christ, the Lord rejoiced in his insight, and then made this promise: "I will build my church, and the gates of Hades (Hell) will not prevail over it" (Matthew 16:18). Later, He commissioned His followers to go everywhere and make disciples, sending them on their way with a promise: "Surely I will be with you always, to the very end of the age" (28:20). That's two clear promises from the Lord—the promise to prevail and the promise of His presence.

Yet I find a lot of Christians today who doubt these commitments. Apparently, they are not convinced that Christ will build His church, because they assume that people will not even listen to the Gospel. Furthermore, they are not convinced that Christ is really with them, because they feel so alone in the presence of unbelievers. As a result, they do not sow seeds of faith because they do not expect faith to sprout. Result? Faith does not sprout. And how can it? As Paul asked, "How can they believe in the one of whom they have not heard? And how can they hear without someone preaching to them?" (Romans 10:14).

Fortunately, there are some who take the Lord at His word. Norm Miller is one of those. Norm is the chief executive officer of Interstate Batteries, which markets the number one replacement battery in the United States. When it comes to the gospel, Norm takes Christ's promises seriously. Not only does he share his faith at every opportunity, he has used Interstate as a platform from which to reach others.

For example, Interstate headquarters is located in north Dallas, a part of North Texas that has experienced rapid growth in recent years. As Norm saw people flooding into the area, he asked, "What are we doing to reach these people with the good news about Christ?" So he asked Jim Coté, Interstate's corporate chaplain, whether any ministry was actively engaged in door-to-door evangelism in the area.

"What we found out," Jim says, "was that no one was doing that anymore because no one believed it was effective. But Norm—who knows an awful lot about sales and marketing—pointed out that if no one was doing it, no one could say whether it worked or didn't work. Maybe it wasn't working because no one was trying to make it work."

So Interstate hired an evangelist and developed a short-term campaign for him to go door-to-door with the Gospel. Result? A modest number of people came to Christ, many of whom would never have heard the Gospel otherwise. Did it cause a citywide revival? No, but the response was enough to confirm that Norm's faith in God was not misplaced. The Lord was building His church!

God always honors faith. He always deals severely with unbelief. He certainly did in Samaria. No sooner had Elisha's prophecy of plenty left his lips than the king's right-hand man piped up and said, in effect, "No way! Even if God dropped food out of heaven, what you say can't happen" (2 Kings 7:2). Thus he directly contradicted Elisha, turning "Thus saith the Lord" into "Thus saith *not* the Lord."

Only one of the two men could be right. But they were engaged in something far more serious than predicting who would win the Super Bowl. This was a matter of life and death. First of all, the fate of the city was hanging in the balance. Moreover, Elisha's life itself was on the line—not from the king's threat, but from the requirements of the Old Testament Law.

As a prophet, Elisha had no room for error. He had to be accurate one hundred percent of the time. Otherwise, the Law said he should be put to death for representing himself as a bona fide messenger from the Lord (Deuteronomy 18:20). Talk about working without a net! Can you imagine if we applied that standard today to those who claim to speak for God? I wonder how many pulpits would suddenly become vacant? You see, we've got too many people signing checks with God's name. Their claims sound wonderful; unfortunately, they are fraudulent. In the end, they discredit the name of the Lord.

At any rate, someone was now challenging Elisha's prediction of food beyond measure. Interestingly, the Law also said that if anyone refused to heed the words of a prophet claiming to speak for the Lord, God would call him to account (18:19). So the king's officer had placed himself in jeopardy by his sarcastic put-down of Elisha. The prophet declared what his fate would be: "You will see it with your own eyes, but you will not eat any of it!" (2 Kings 7:2).

The lesson for us here is not that we should go around making extravagant claims about what God will or won't do, and then delivering ultimatums to people who doubt our words. That would be a ministry of condemnation, not multiplication. No, God has called us to declare, with integrity and honesty, the plain truth of the Gospel and its implications, and then let people decide for themselves. In doing so, we will inevitably encounter unbelief. For instance, people will try to discredit the Bible. They will doubt the reality of miracles. Some will even argue against the existence of God Himself. There will be many points of contention.

When we run into those, we should stridently defend our faith without attacking those who question our faith. We should argue *for* the Gospel, not *with* our opponents. We must attack lies, not people. We may renounce their ideas, but we must respect their right to believe—or disbelieve—as they wish. This is the approach that Paul recommended. "By setting forth the truth plainly we commend ourselves to every man's conscience in the sight of God" (2 Corinthians 2:4).

"But what if they just won't believe?" someone may be asking. Then all we can do is remain patient and pray—pray that God's light will somehow penetrate their darkness. That's why Paul went on, "Even if our gospel is veiled, it is veiled to those who are perishing. The god of this age has blinded the minds of unbelievers, so that they cannot see the light of the gospel of the glory of Christ" (4:3–4).

God never forces anyone to accept His truth. So there's no point in our trying to browbeat people into faith, or to denounce them when they resist God's Word. Elisha didn't do that with the officer. He knew that it was God's prerogative to deal with that man's unbelief.

Faith Is the Victory!

In the end, of course, the Lord always proves Himself faithful. Second Kings 7 records His victory over the Arameans and His vindication in the eyes of His people. If you've ever wondered whether God has a sense of humor, you need to read this passage. It's a classic! It is freighted with irony and comedy, all of it designed to show not only that the Lord is God, but that He is Savior as well.

First God routs the Arameans. By miraculously causing the sound of a great army in the night, He panics the army and sends it running for home (2 Kings 7:6–7). In fact, they leave their clothing and equipment strewn all along the way (7:15). Remember the highway from Kuwait to Baghdad after the Iraqis retreated from Kuwait in the Gulf War? They left abandoned tanks, jeeps, and other equipment for miles along that roadway. That's what the road from Samaria to Damascus looked like.

This victory served as a rebuke to the Israelite king. Recall that he had given up on God in disgust. Now he had egg on his face—and the Lord made sure that everyone recognized it as egg! First, He appointed four lepers to discover the Arameans' withdrawal and bring that wonderful news to the city (7:3–11).

I'm always amazed at God's choice of His messengers. So often He uses outcasts, such as these lepers, to spread good news. These men were the bottom feeders of society. They had nothing to lose (7:3–4). Perhaps for that reason, they were the most open to taking risks. So they walked into the Aramean camp—and found it completely deserted!

The account gives us some idea of their mental state at that moment: "They ate and drank, and carried away silver, gold and clothes, and went off and hid them. They returned and entered another tent and took some things from it and hid them also" (7:8). In other words, they probably thought they had died and gone to heaven!

But eventually, their consciences caught up with them. "They said to each other, 'We're not doing right. This is a day of good news and we are keeping it to ourselves." So they decide to go and report it to the palace (7:9).

I think the Holy Spirit ensured that this statement would be recorded here as a goad to us believers within shouting distance of the twenty-first century. How many of us are keeping the good news to ourselves—running around in our Christian communities, enjoying our Christian friends, listening to our Christian speakers, reading our Christian books, having a field day in our wonderful Christian sub-culture? We are feasting on the spoils of Christ's victory on the cross. Meanwhile, people all around us are dying of spiritual starvation.

May I ask you what may be a rather disturbing question? How many unbelievers can you count among your *personal* friends? I'm finding more and more Christians who are forced to answer, "None!" Is that what Christ would have us do?

"Oh, but Brother Hendricks, you don't understand," someone may reply. "I don't make friends with non-Christians, because I don't want to be corrupted." To which I say, you may not be corrupted, but you also will not be fruitful.

As Christ's followers, we are not to be of the world, but we are still to be in the world. We are to be in the world in order that we might win the world. And winning people to Christ occurs most naturally and effectively within the context of personal relationships. As one person has well put it, one beggar telling another beggar where to find food.

The lepers returned to the city, and the good news made its way to the king. The ruler refused to believe what he was hearing. He was certain there was some trickery involved. But after he sent a handful of men on a suicide mission to find out, they returned and confirmed the lepers' tale. With that, the people went streaming out of the city, and Elisha's word to the king came to pass (7:11–16).

With the Arameans routed and the king rebuked, all that remained was for God to exact retribution from the officer for his unbelief. What happened to this man is the climax of the passage. Notice that the account emphasizes his outcome by placing it at the end of the chapter; by devoting four verses to reporting it; by repeating word for word Elisha's prophecy of plentiful food, the officer's denial that it would happen, and Elisha's prediction that he would see it but not taste of it; and by throwing in the editorial comment, "And that is exactly what happened to him, for the people trampled him in the gateway, and he died" (7:17–20). The point? There is nothing more fatal than unbelief!

On the other hand, there is nothing more victorious than faith. That's crucial to remember as you seek to bear fruit as a follower of Christ. You will invariably run into opposition—whether the fiery wrath of people's anger, or the cold water of people's doubt. In either case, your challenge is to hold fast to what God has said. "This is the victory that has overcome the world," John wrote, "even our faith" (1 John 5:4).

PART THREE

Leaving
a
Legacy

CHAPTER THIRTEEN

Making a Difference, Impacting Lives

I am now in my fourth decade of teaching at the graduate school level. For the first thirty years, I devoted my efforts to the subject of Christian education—the art and science of training people as followers of Christ. More recently, I have concentrated on leadership, in the belief that what the church—and the world—need more than anything else today are people equipped to lead. Underlying both of these emphases, as a principle and as a personal practice, has always been the theme of mentoring, that subtle but powerful relationship in which one person can literally alter the course of another person's life.

As you can tell, I am committed to the idea that God has put His people here for influence. I can accept that some will have more influence than others, and that each will influence differently from others. But I will never be persuaded that God wants any of us to slink onto the stage of history, live out our days, and quietly make an exit without in any way making a contribution to this world, both for time and eternity.

On what basis do I make such a claim? As always, the measure of meaning must be taken from the Word of God. In the end, that is our only reliable reference for reality. Turning, then, to Paul's epistle to the Ephesians, we find that God had purposes in mind for each one of us before we were ever created (Ephesians 1:3–14). Furthermore, God has ensured that those purposes will be carried out, because He has saved us "by grace through faith" (2:8). And then Paul comes to the practical end toward which all of this is directed: "For we are God's workmanship, created in Christ Jesus to do good works, which God prepared in advance for us to do" (2:10).

There it is: We have been created in Christ Jesus to do good works—works that God has *prepared* for us to do. There is a reason for our being here. God has an intention for our lives, yours and mine. He has prepared us, called us, saved us, gifted us—to make a difference in this world, to make an *impact*.

Unfortunately, I'm afraid too many believers have lost sight of that vision. Some are convinced that they can't make a difference. Others have decided they don't need to. As a result, they have folded their hands and become spectators—and ultimately captives—of the times. Instead of being the influencers, they become the influenced. Instead of setting the pace, they are lucky to keep up with it.

I am somewhat resigned to that fact. I have come to realize that this side of heaven, there will always be more people wanting to be led than there will be leaders willing to lead. That was true in the days of the prophets; it is still true today.

But if you are among that rare breed of individuals who are awake to God's call; if, like the boy Samuel, you are saying to Him, "Speak, LORD, for your servant is listening" (1 Samuel 3:9–10); if, like Isaiah, you are willing to throw open your life to God's plans and purposes with the words, "Here am I. Send me!" (Isaiah 6:8); if you are intent on really going for broke in terms of using your life strategically to accomplish God's purposes—then this chapter is for you.

I want to suggest four principles from Elijah and Elisha about impacting our world today. These men not only changed their generation, they left a legacy for generations to come. How were they able to exert such influence? And what lessons can we draw from their experience that will transfer to our own? Here are four observations to provoke your thinking.

1. If we want to leave a lasting impact, we must confront our culture as we find it, not as we would like it to be. Have you ever played the game in your mind of imagining the era of history in which you would most liked to have lived? Perhaps you are drawn to those ancient days of Abraham, those seminal years in which faith in the Lord was finding its focus. Or perhaps you think about the golden ages of the Greeks or the Romans, during which the foundations of Western civilization were being laid. Perhaps you prefer the Renaissance, when art and literature reached what some consider their highest expression. Or perhaps you would have been most comfortable in colonial America, when the United States was born amid the tumult of patriotic rhetoric and impassioned sacrifice.

These fantasies are fun to play out in one's mind. Sometimes they can prove instructive. But our challenge is always to live today, not yesterday. To do that, we have to become as adept at studying our own times as we are at studying history. We must appreciate the world around us for what it is, not for what we would like it to be.

Let me give an illustration that hits close to home for me as a Bible teacher. One time I was leading a Bible study, and we were working our way through the Gospel of Mark. Our passage for one particular session was at the end of Mark 4, which gives an account of Jesus stilling the storm on the Sea of Galilee. I was about half-way through the hour when a woman in the group raised her hand and said, "Hold it! Just exactly where is this incident taking place?"

"On the Sea of Galilee," I replied.

"Yeah, I know, but where's that?" she asked.

"It's in the northern part of Palestine," I said, and started to reach for a map.

"Yes, but where is Palestine?" she went on, her frustration mounting. She was totally serious.

I was totally shocked. You see, this woman was no dullard. She happened to have a Ph.D.! And I thought to myself, "How in the world did she get this far without knowing where Palestine was?" Then it dawned on me: we now have a generation of people for whom the Bible is a closed book. Basic Bible knowledge that I and my contemporaries used to take for granted is now considered specialized knowledge!

All the statistics bear this out. Despite the fact that almost every home in America has at least one Bible, pollster George Gallup has found that not even half of adults can name even one of the four Gospels. Fewer than half know who delivered the Sermon on the Mount, or that Jesus had twelve disciples, or even (despite centuries of the celebration of Christmas) that He was born at Bethlehem. In short, countless people in our society are now functionally illiterate in terms of a basic understanding of Scripture. As sociologist Miriam Murphy has noted, many have "a Ph.D. in aerodynamics, but only a third grade knowledge of religion."

I could wish things were different. I could lament this depressing state of affairs. I could lash out at all the parents and Sunday school teachers and educators who ought to have been drilling biblical facts into young people's heads throughout this century. I could do all of these things and more. But what good would it do? If I want to have an impact, I've got to start with where people are at, and build on that. I've got to assume that when it comes to the Bible, most people are working with no information—or worse, misinformation. So I've got to explain, clarify, and provide meaning. Otherwise, I have little hope of influencing their lives. I'll just come off as one more irrelevant elitist from the ivory tower.

Elijah and Elisha had it a lot worse. They were sent to a society that was committed, heart and soul, to rebellion against the Lord. Israel was not a secular society; it was an apostate society. It actually had a memory of the Lord, but given the nation's spiritual condition, that memory was like a bad hangover.

To recap the situation (speaking of basic Bible knowledge): God had brought His people the Israelites out of slavery in Egypt and settled them in the Promised Land of Canaan. Eventually He gave them a king, David. David was succeeded by Solomon, and Solomon by his son Rehoboam. But Rehoboam was a harsh ruler, and shortly after he assumed the throne, rebellion broke out. Ten northern tribes seceded and formed their own kingdom, called Israel. Their king was named Jeroboam. The two tribes that remained under Rehoboam, Judah and Benjamin, became known as Judah.

You might think that God would have chosen sides in this dispute, but He did not. In fact, He offered Jeroboam a lasting dynasty, as long as he and his descendants followed the Lord (1 Kings 11:37–38). Yet remarkably, Jeroboam departed from the Lord and turned to idolatry almost from the start of his reign. Moreover, every king who followed him also "did evil in the eyes of the Lord," as Scripture puts it. There was not a single one who repented and returned to God.

This, then, was the environment in which Elijah and Elisha operated. By the time they came along, the culture was steeped in the worship of Baal, one of the principal gods of the pagan peoples living in and around Israel. Baal-worship was essentially a fertility cult. Its practices, which included ritual prostitution, were intended to coax the gods into blessing crops and livestock.

Baal-worship also lacked a moral foundation, and therefore offered nothing to check immorality and corruption. As a result, the Israelites sunk to a lower moral plain than the Canaanites whom they had dispossessed. Like the Canaanites, they ended up with a two-tiered society, with extremely wealthy and powerful aristocrats on top, and a large citizenry of impoverished farmers on the bottom. With each successive king, evil became further entrenched, and the memory of the Lord slipped a bit further into oblivion.

Now imagine if it were your assignment to make an impact for God in that culture. What would be your strategy? Where would you start? I can tell you where Elijah and Elisha started. First they developed a strong grasp of the Word of God. Then they developed a keen understanding of their society. Then they went into action.

The order is crucial. First they came to grips with what God had to say about the nation. You see, Israel's moral and spiritual decline did not catch the Lord by surprise. Centuries earlier, He had foreseen what might happen. He even told Moses what He would do about it if it did: "I will break down your stubborn pride and make the sky above you like iron and the ground beneath you like bronze. Your strength will be spent in vain, because your soil will not yield its crops, nor will the trees of the land yield their fruit" (Leviticus 26:19–20). God intended these famine conditions not so much as a punishment, but as a corrective measure to draw His people back to Him.

Elijah knew that. He was a student of the Word. In fact, when the Lord told him to go to Ahab and declare that the rains would cease (1 Kings 17:1), I believe the prophet was *expecting* that assignment. God had given fair warning; thus it was only a matter of time before He let His judgment fall.

But Elijah and Elisha were also students of their society. They didn't cloister themselves away in denial and ignorance. They faced squarely the realities of their times. For instance, it is evident that Elijah was an expert on Baal-worship. His encounter with the 450 prophets of Baal on Mount Carmel bears that out. He knew what they believed, how they were motivated, and what their rituals and incantations meant. Most importantly, he knew where they stood in the eyes of the people, and what it would take to break their hold over the Israelites' hearts and minds.

When you put together an understanding of what God has said with an understanding of how a society functions, you are then prepared to take action. This was the pattern of the prophets. Every one of their activities reported in Scripture was freighted with significance. They were always applying God's truth to the problems of the day. Their faith did not exist in a vacuum. It was a tool—sometimes even a weapon—for working in and on their culture.

That's the art we need to cultivate today—the art of placing the finger of God's truth on the nerve of societal need. Oh, we have Bible scholars aplenty. But as a professional in biblical studies, I'm compelled to say that many of us increasingly find ourselves in the embarrassing position of answering questions that no one is asking. Meanwhile, we have sociologists and others doing a splendid job of critiquing our culture, giving excellent diagnoses of what is wrong. But when it comes to prescribing a cure, they invariably have more questions than they have answers.

And so we need a synthesis. We need people who can look at the Word and look at the world and find a correlation. I like the way John Stott has put it: it's easy to be biblical without being contemporary, and it is easy to be contemporary without being biblical. But to be biblical and contemporary—that's the art that leads to effective communication.

2. *If we want to leave a lasting impact, our objective must be faithfulness, not success.* We Americans have a mania for success. We also tend to define success in a very narrow way. But I submit that what we call "success" is largely a culturally determined value, and that the rest of the world, both today and down through history, has not been nearly as enamored of that value as we are.

That should give us cause to pause. What does everyone else know that we don't? Is it possible that Americans are pursuing, individually and collectively, something that is totally without merit or meaning?

I raise this question because when we talk about making an impact on the world, we are bound to interpret that objective through the lens of our own culturally influenced background. For the typical American, "making an impact" suggests starting something new, or getting up on a platform, or raising money, or changing the political system—activities whose "success" can be quantified and measured.

I certainly wouldn't take away from the necessity and value of those things. But I would point out they are heavily dependent on circumstance. That is, not everyone will be able—or interested—to have an "impact" in those kinds of ways. In fact, if we consider the world as a whole, relatively few people will. Therefore, if God wants His people to make a difference, then "making a difference" must mean something more than developing a "successful" program or system.

Let me put it another way. Having read this far, you may be thinking, "I can't make an impact. I have nothing to offer. Hendricks is talking about studying the Bible and studying the culture and making a synthesis. Why, I don't even know what a 'synthesis' is! I'm just trying to live my life as best I can in a way that honors the Lord. Sure, I want my life to count. But all I have to offer is what I am—that and a little bit of faith."

To which I say, you got it! That's it! That's exactly what God is looking for—an available individual who is willing to exercise a little bit of faith in using what God has given him. Making an impact is not any more complicated than that.

Does the fact that we are using Elijah and Elisha—two of the greatest prophets in Israel's history—put you off? Is their example a bit too intimidating? Then consider this: their greatness is seen primarily in *retrospect*, not in prospect. We read about their exploits today with a sense of awe and wonder. But do you know where they stood at the time? They were not in the center of the action. They were assigned to God's "Plan B." Let me explain.

A moment ago I mentioned that the northern kingdom of Israel was a rebel state. It had broken off from Judah, which continued to be governed by the descendants of David. Israel never did recover from its apostasy. In fact, God eventually allowed the Assyrians to come in and wipe it out. The survivors were mostly resettled to Assyria, where they were largely absorbed into that pagan society. A handful remained in Canaan, where they intermarried with other peoples and became the Samaritans, about whom we read so much in the New Testament.

Thus the primary focus of God's plan seems to have rested on the southern kingdom of Judah. Judah also went into captivity, but its people by and large retained their Jewish heritage. In fact, God preserved Judah in order to bring about the birth of Jesus.

Where did that leave Elijah and Elisha? The answer is, they were agents in an alternative plan. They were sent to a kingdom that was outside of God's will and never did return to it. What does this say, then, about the "success" of the prophets' efforts? They were temporarily "successful" at beating back the forces of idolatry and wickedness. But if their goal was to return the kingdom to righteousness, and perhaps even reconcile it to its brother Judah, then we are forced to admit that they failed, because that never happened.

At least, that might be an American interpretation of the record. To a success-minded American, the ministries of Elijah and Elisha could easily come off as well-intentioned, but ultimately futile. After all, they didn't yield "results."

But I'm convinced that God sees things differently. One primary clue comes from the apostle Paul's statement to the Corinthians about how they should regard his own work: "Men ought to regard us as servants of Christ and as those entrusted with the secret things of God" (1 Corinthians 4:1). A servant of Christ, entrusted with the secret things of God—sounds a lot like Elijah and Elisha!

But Paul goes on: "Now it is required that those who have been given a trust must prove faithful" (4:2). What a remarkable statement! Paul doesn't say that a servant—a person charged with a trust—must prove "successful." He must prove *faithful*. He must fulfill his trust. That may or may not mean big results.

That is also the lesson of Jesus' parable of the talents (Matthew 25:14–20). Perhaps you recall the tale. A wealthy man goes on a journey, but before he leaves he gives a sum of money to three different "servants," or managers. To one manager he gives five talents, to the second, two talents, and to the third, one talent. His instructions are to do business with the money and make a profit.

Again, Americans tend to focus on the *results*, on the *amount* of money each manager gained or failed to gain. The first one doubled his money, resulting in ten talents. Likewise, the second doubled his money, resulting in four talents. The third did nothing with his share, resulting in one talent.

When the master returned, he took note of the profits, or lack thereof. But his evaluation of performance focused on *faithfulness*, not financial gain. To the two responsible managers, he said, "Well, done, *good and faithful* servant! You have been *faithful* with a few things; I will put you in charge of many things" (25:21, 23, emphasis added). But he called the unproductive manager "wicked," "lazy," and "worthless" (25:26, 30).

Don't misunderstand—I'm as keen on results as the next person. But I'm also keenly aware that results, particularly in the spiritual realm, are largely outside our control. Too many other factors affect the outcome. Therefore, we would be wise to give up inflated notions of "success," if we have them, and concentrate instead on faithfully carrying out the tasks to which God has called us, in the circumstances where He has placed us—*and then leave the results to Him*.

There are three benefits to adopting this attitude. First, it protects us against thinking too highly of ourselves. This is a severe temptation when we start talking about making an impact on society. Is it not a bit arrogant to think that we will make some great, lasting contribution? But if "success" is our mandate, that's exactly what we will tend to think.

If, however, our focus is on faithfulness, then we can relax about altering the course of history and concentrate on today. That's all that God has given us—today, not tomorrow. Therefore, our overarching concern ought not to be for the future, but on what we are we *today*, to make *today* count for Him. Obviously, planning for and paying attention to the future are vital. But at the end of the day, we will be found faithful if we can say, "This day was worthwhile, because I carried out God's purposes for me."

The second benefit of concentrating on faithfulness is just the opposite: it protects us against thinking too lowly of ourselves. This is a temptation if you feel that you have nothing to offer. "I'm not a teacher." "I'm not a leader." "I'm not a scholar." "I haven't had much education." I've heard all the excuses.

But I'm here to tell you that if you are in Christ, you have all that you need to make a significant difference with your life. You may need to cultivate the resources God has given you. But He has not placed you on the planet by accident. He has given you at least some abilities and opportunities. He has given you at least some relationships. He has given you at least some awareness that your life ought to matter—otherwise you wouldn't be reading this chapter. Take whatever He has given you and make it your ambition to use it for His glory. He will honor your faithfulness.

However, thinking too lowly of oneself can relate not only to one's person, but to one's position. I often encounter this among students of mine after they have graduated from the seminary. I'll run into a guy three or four years after he's taken a pastorate, and I can hardly recognize him! He's got a face so long it looks like a frontispiece to the Book of Lamentations!

So I ask him why, and he complains that he feels like he's wasting his talents. Then he tells me about his church. It's not exactly what he had hoped for; in fact, it's a far cry from it. As we talk, I discover that his image of a "significant" pastorate is a large church in a major metropolitan area, from which he broadcasts a widely hailed radio or television ministry, and his pronouncements are regularly picked up by the media. Because he doesn't have anything approaching that—and frankly, little prospect of ever having it—he feels like a failure.

But the premise of his thinking is flawed. He thinks that making a difference for God has to do with one's *place*, rather than one's performance. He needs to realize that many of God's choicest servants have labored in obscurity—in homes, in factories, in inner cities, in jails, in trackless deserts, on wide-open seas. Their contributions may have been unnoted by humanity, but they will not be overlooked by God.

I suppose most of us would like to feel that we're at the center of the action. But that is God's choice, not ours. He has plans for some of us to serve in the backwaters, in the places where few will ever recognize our efforts—or, like Elijah and Elisha, where righteousness is not and never will be honored. Can we make an impact there? Yes, so long as we carry out God's intentions. The issue is not *where* we serve, but *when* we serve. Our Master is not asking us to be famous, but faithful.

Finally, focusing on faithfulness helps us think *rightly* about ourselves. The main pitfall of living with the "success syndrome" is comparing ourselves with others. That's always perilous. God will never ask you why you were not as successful, or even as faithful, as someone else. He will only ask you why you did or did not carry out his assignment for you. He will not ask you why you were not Elijah or Elisha. He will ask you why you were not you.

3. *If we want to leave a lasting impact, we must take the long view, not the quick fix.* Just as our first impulse as Americans is to seek for success, our second is to look for immediate results. When we want change, we want it right away.

But there is no such thing as instant impact. From the divine perspective, significance is not measured in years or even decades, but in lives and generations. At least, that would appear to be the case with Israel.

When Elijah first appeared on the scene, King Ahab was on the throne. Ahab is believed to have ruled for twenty-two years, between 874 and 852 B.C. He was succeeded by his son Ahaziah, and some believe that Elijah was translated to heaven about the time of Ahaziah's death. That would have been about 850 B.C. Elisha then became the main prophet to Israel, and he lived perhaps into his eighties, dying during the reign of Jehoash (801–786 B.C.).

Thus we have an eighty-eight-year window during which these prophets lived and worked. In the scope of biblical history, that's a relatively short amount of time. Yet much was accomplished. At the beginning of Elijah's ministry, there were 450 prophets of Baal installed by Ahab and Jezebel, as well as 400 other prophets dedicated to Asherah, another pagan deity. Almost everyone who remained loyal to the Lord was in hiding. But by the time of Elisha's death, the entire family of Ahab had been removed, Jezebel had been put to death, a school for the prophets had been built at Jericho, and Israel was holding its own against its long-time nemesis, the kingdom of Aram.

As I've indicated, the nation never did turn back wholly to the Lord. In fact, the brief revivals that Elijah and Elisha witnessed were the last gasp of Israel's spirituality. Within a few short years (722 B.C.), Assyria invaded, Samaria was sacked, and the people were taken into exile.

But looking at this history, the remarkable thing is not that these two great men of God were unable to accomplish more, but that they were able to accomplish anything at all! They were drilling into rock-hard rebelliousness. Every king they encountered opposed them. Almost every move they made met with resistance. So if we wonder why they did not sow more seeds of faith, we must consider that they had to blast through granite just to break up the soil!

Still, much was accomplished during their combined seventy or more years of work. I could wish that more of us today had that long-term perspective. Perhaps we underestimate the task.

I sit on a number of boards of Christian organizations, so I have a front row seat on some of the exciting things that God is doing in our day. But then I'll hear someone say, "Hey, isn't your group working with young people? I just read the other day that adolescents are having pre-marital sex in record numbers. What are you guys doing about that? It seems as if you're losing ground!"

When I hear that type of thing, I'm just appalled at the short-sighted thinking it reveals. I want to say, "Friend, did it ever occur to you that this problem didn't just flare up yesterday? Our society has been throwing sex at young people for most of this century—and more now than ever before. What made you think that one organization, which is only a few years old, is by itself going to reverse that problem overnight?"

If we want to see significant impact, we've got to commit ourselves to the long haul. But I sometimes wonder whether American Christians have the discipline to do that? Are we willing to stay the course for the twenty, forty, eighty, or more years that it takes to grow a seedling into a mature tree that bears fruit year in and year out?

One thing that might help is to commit ourselves to principles rather than to programs. Programs come and go (or ought to) according to the need of the times. By contrast, principles have staying power. They sink down to the bedrock of truth.

British politician Tony Brenn puts it this way. "There are kings and there are prophets. The kings have the power and the prophets have the principles." That's an intriguing observation in light of our study of Elijah and Elisha. They faced kings who seemed so powerful. Yet their power was invariably short-lived. Elisha outlived five kings. More importantly, the principles for which he stood outlived his nation—as well as the nation that swallowed his nation up. In fact, the last time I checked, those principles are still in operation today!

The lesson is that power tends to change rapidly, while enduring principles last over time—and eternal principles last forever. So it's worth asking: what are you relying on to make an impact that will live on after you're gone?

4. *If we want to leave a lasting impact, we must never forget that God never gives up on His people.* Making a difference in the lives of others sounds like a noble task—and it is. But it's also hard work, and at times it can be frustrating, if not downright discouraging. People can let us down, they can turn away, they can turn against us, they can turn against the Lord. In moments like these, it's easy to throw up our hands and say, "What's the use?"

I've had my share of those disappointments. There have been times when I thought I was really affecting the life of another individual in a positive, Christlike way, only to discover that instead of having influence, I was actually being ignored. That really shot holes in my confidence. It also made me wonder, "Does anyone *care* about the things of the Lord? If not, why am I putting myself through this?"

You can see that for someone who wants to make an impact, the worst thing to happen is a lack of response. That really tests one's mettle!

It's hard to say exactly when Elijah and Elisha faced that challenge. Perhaps for Elijah, it was when Jezebel put out an all-points bulletin to have the prophet rubbed out (1 Kings 19:2). It may be that after his experience on Mount Carmel, he had hoped she would fall to her knees in repentance and affirm what her people had affirmed: "The Lord—he is God! The Lord— he is God!" (18:39). Instead, her rage against the Lord—and the prophet—only burned more brightly.

Perhaps for Elisha, the sense of hitting a brick wall came when his servant Gehazi lied to Naaman and extracted silver and clothing out of him (2 Kings 5:22–23). Remember that for years, Elisha had been

Elijah's faithful servant. In fact, it was through that association that he was groomed to become Elijah's successor. It seems plausible that Elisha had similar hopes for Gehazi. Now, Gehazi had disqualified himself from service, and he was sent away in disgrace (5:26-27).

Sooner or later, anyone who wants to make a difference for God is bound to wonder, "What difference am I making?" If the answer seems to be, "Not much," it's quite tempting to throw in the towel.

But here is where the account of the prophets offers tremendous hope. For their lives and ministry are a profound testimony to the fact that while people may give up on God, He does not give up on them. His grace endures.

Therefore, we need to endure. We need to hang in there with people, praying for them, working with them, standing up under their opposition, just as the prophets did—and just as Jesus did, too. Aren't you glad that He did not give up on you and me?

When Elisha died, he was buried in an unmarked tomb. Scripture records that shortly thereafter, a group of Israelites was burying a man nearby. During the preparation of his tomb, a band of Moabite raiders approached. Terrified, the Israelites stopped their work on the new tomb, opened Elisha's tomb, and threw the man's body inside. When the body touched Elisha's bones, the man returned to life (13:21).

Have you touched Elisha's bones? Or, like most of the Israelites, are you dead in terms of your spiritual condition? The power is not in the bones, the power is in the One who gives life to the bones. May His power operate through you, so that you will make a significant, lasting impact in this generation, and in generations to come.

AKNOWLEDGEMENTS

N
o doubt you have heard of the proverbial cat that will not go away. The original seeds for *Standing Together* are found in the little paperback *Elijah, Confrontation, Conflict and Crisis* that I put out many years ago. Actually that material has seen several titles and printings, so I was satisfied that the material had served its purpose well and I thought it was time I put it to rest..

Then about a year ago, I got a phone call from John Van Diest of Vision House Publishing. John has been a long-time friend and a favorite co-conspirator on numerous adventures in the faith. I have always had the utmost respect for his superlative work in publishing. But when he asked about my Elijah material, I thought he had gone into the antique business! "What in the world would he want with that" I wondered.

But true to form, John had come up with an idea that was as brilliant as it was obvious: to revise the Elijah material for the Nineties and add to it the sequel to the story—the life of Elisha. After all, John pointed out, I have been championing the theme of mentoring in recent years. Why not present Elijah and Elisha back-to-back, as a biblical model of mentoring for a new generation?

I could not say no to that idea. But I was forced to say no to the execution of the idea, for I was covered over with commitments. However, John has not survived in publishing as long as he has by allowing the schedules of busy authors to hold him hostage! As soon as I agreed that this book ought to be written, he sprang into action and matched me up with a talented writer named Chip McGregor. Chip took a handful of my seed thoughts and cultivated them into a mature harvest of words, sentences, paragraphs, and chapters. Without that invaluable spade work, this book might never have seen the light of day.

Once a manuscript was produced, the next step was to have it edited. The name that immediately came to mind, both for John and for me, was Bill, my younger son. In addition to working with a wide variety of clients as a consultant in communication, Bill has authored or coauthored about a dozen books, two of which he wrote with me (*Living By the Book*, and *As Iron Sharpens Iron*). I was overjoyed when Bill agreed to help us with *Standing Together*, because he so understands my personality and style. His expertise has been like the booster engine of a rocket, thrusting this book into an orbit I never imagined it could achieve.

One other member of the "flight crew" deserves special honor. My wife Jeanne has been involved with this material for as long as I have. In fact, a good case could be made for the idea that the original book on Elijah would never have come about apart from her presence in my life. She has been both a witness to and participant in the long-term history of this project. Somehow I think she knew all along that this particular cat was a "keeper." It might doze and roam, as cats will do, but it would never go away!